BONES

ON THE

GROUND

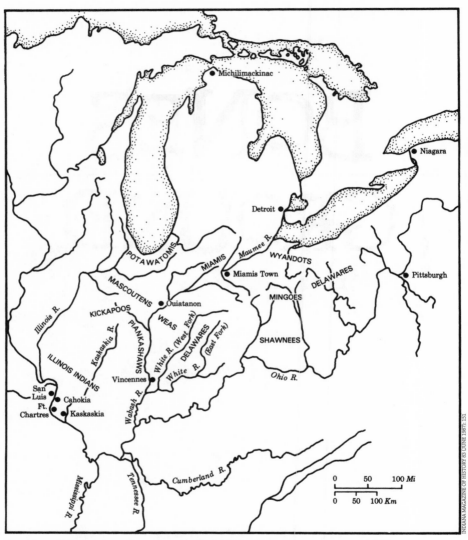

Location of Native American tribes in the Old Northwest Territory, circa 1777.

BONES ON THE GROUND

ELIZABETH O'MALEY

Bones on the Ground is made possible
through the generous support of the
Mississinewa Battlefield Society.

Indiana Historical Society Press | Indianapolis 2014

© 2014 Indiana Historical Society Press

This book is a publication of the
Indiana Historical Society Press
Eugene and Marilyn Glick Indiana History Center
450 West Ohio Street
Indianapolis, Indiana 45202-3269 USA
www.indianahistory.org
Telephone orders 1-800-447-1830
Fax orders 1-317-234-0562
Online orders @ http://shop.indianahistory.org

O'Maley, Elizabeth.
Bones on the ground / Elizabeth O'Maley.
pages cm
Audience: Age 13 to 17.
Includes bibliographical references.
ISBN 978-0-87195-362-9 (cloth : alkaline paper)
1. Indians of North America—Wars—Northwest, Old—Juvenile literature. 2. Indians of North America—Northwest, Old—History—Juvenile literature. 3. Indians of North America—Northwest, Old—Government relations—Juvenile literature. 4. Indians of North America—Northwest, Old—Biography—Juvenile literature. 5. Indians, Treatment of—History—Juvenile literature. 6. Frontier and pioneer life—Northwest, Old—Juvenile literature. 7. Northwest, Old—History—1775-1865—Juvenile literature. 8. Northwest, Old—History, Military—Juvenile literature. 9. Northwest, Old—Race relations—History—Juvenile literature. I. Title.
    E81.O45 2014
    970.004'97—dc23
                    2014020097

⊗ The paper in this publication meets the minimum requirements of
American National Standard for Information Sciences—Permanence of Paper for Printed
Library Materials, ANSI Z39. 48–1984

For Isaac and Salma, their Grandpa, their Mommy and Daddy,
their aunts and uncles. I love you all very much.
May the generations always hold hands.

Table of Contents

Preface

The idea for this book was born one day in 1955 when I came upon an Indian arrowhead in my family's garden in Ohio. I knew Indians had dined with the pilgrims in Massachusetts and fought Davy Crockett of Tennessee. But I did not know they had roamed the very ground on which I was standing. It thrilled me to know it had once been home to people who hunted with bows and arrows.

Two years earlier my hometown had celebrated its 120th birthday and Ohio's sesquicentennial. Men grew beards and women wore bonnets to honor the town's first residents. My arrowhead showed that others had come before them—Indians had lived here! Why had they vanished, leaving only their pieces of flint behind? What had happened to the Indians?

One of the first white children born in our town was Henry Church Jr., who became a blacksmith and an artist of great merit. People from Cleveland, Ohio, came to Chagrin Falls by horse and buggy to purchase the sculptures displayed in his yard. After 1885 many traveled on to a secluded spot by the river a few miles out from town, where Church had carved puzzling images on a giant chunk of glacial rock. Every evening for many months he had worked by lantern light in the still, dark woods.

Because one face of the boulder displayed an Indian woman encircled by a large serpent, it became known as "Squaw Rock." A quiver of arrows, an eagle, a dog, and a papoose were shown with the woman. On another side of the rock Church carved tall ships, a frontiersman with an ax, a log cabin, and the U.S. Capitol.

As a teenager I often hiked to Squaw Rock and occasionally paused to ponder the artist's meaning. I learned that Church had called his work "The Rape of the Indians by the White Man." He intended to portray the passing of the Indians as American "civilization" pushed westward.

Bones on the Ground elaborates on his vision. It depicts people and events that answer my childhood question: What happened to the Indians? I hope the collage of stories in this book builds a coherent narrative of the Indians' struggle to hold their ground.

While researching the lives of people in this book, conflicting portraits emerged. Was William Wells a corrupt opportunist or a courageous hero? Was the Shawnee Prophet a power-hungry charlatan or a devoutly religious man? Did Little Turtle or Blue Jacket command the warriors who handed the American army its worst defeat?

The answers depend on who's telling the story. For this reason I have let the major characters in *Bones on the Ground* speak for themselves. Like most people, they tend to present themselves in a favorable light, bending and stretching the truth to fit their own views of themselves and the world. Despite possible inaccuracies, I believe that looking from varying perspectives helps us to see a more complete picture.

This book covers events in the Old Northwest Territory from the time of the American Revolution through the removal of the Miami from Indiana in 1846. During those years America's Indian policy was formed. The Indians' struggle continued, even into the next century, as white settlers pushed farther west. Some Indians fought the white intruders, while others adopted their ways. In the end, most Indians were unable to hold their ground.

Author atop Squaw Rock outside of Chagrin Falls, Ohio.

Chronology

October 1778	Blue Jacket and Alexander McKee join British colonel Henry Hamilton's campaign to Vincennes
November 1778	Delaware Indians capture Frances Slocum
November 1780	Little Turtle defeats Augustin Mottin de La Balme
March 1782	Gnadenhutten Massacre
June 1782	Burning of William Crawford
March 1784	Capture of William Wells
October 1786	Benjamin Logan raids Shawnee villages, capture of Spemica Lawba, and murder of Chief Moluntha
July 1787	Northwest Territory established
October 1790	Defeat of Josiah Harmar's troops
November 1791	Arthur St. Clair's Defeat
December 1793	Building of Fort Recovery
June 1794	Battle of Fort Recovery
August 1794	Battle of Fallen Timbers
August 1795	Signing of Treaty of Greenville
Spring 1798	Tecumseh establishes village on White River
January 1801	William Henry Harrison moves to Vincennes as governor of the new Indiana Territory
Winter 1801	William Conner begins trading on White River
June 1803	First Treaty of Fort Wayne
Summer 1804	Quaker Philip Dennis operates Little Turtle's Farm School

August 1804	Treaty of Vincennes
October 1804	Treaty of Saint Louis
August 1805	Treaty of Grouseland
February 1806	Execution of Joshua Jr., a Moravian Christian Indian
September 1806	Village established by Tecumseh and the Prophet near Greenville, Ohio
September 1807	Tecumseh and Blue Jacket speak at courthouse in Chillicothe, Ohio
April 1808	Tecumseh and the Prophet establish Prophetstown on Tippecanoe River
September 1809	Second Treaty of Fort Wayne
June 1810	Execution of Leatherlips
August 1810	Tecumseh confronts Harrison at Grouseland
July 1811	Tecumseh's second visit to Harrison
November 1811	Battle of Tippecanoe
June 1812	United States declares war on Great Britain
July 1812	Death of Little Turtle
August 1812	Death of William Wells at evacuation of Fort Dearborn
August 1812	Shawnee James Logan (Spemica Lawba) takes women and children from Fort Wayne to safety in Piqua, Ohio
September 1812	Pigeon Roost Massacre and sieges at Fort Wayne and Fort Harrison
December 1812	Battle of Mississinewa
January 1813	Battle of River Raisin
May 1813	Siege of Fort Meigs

October 1813	Death of Tecumseh at Battle of Thames and tribes surrender to Harrison
October 1818	Treaty of Saint Marys
September 1820	Delaware removal from Indiana and Mekinges and Conner children leave
March 1824	Fall Creek Massacre
May 1830	Indian Removal Act
Summer 1832	Black Hawk War
October 1832	Shawnee removal from Ohio
September 1833	Treaty of Chicago
September 1837	Frances Slocum reunited with white family
September 1838	Potawatomi Trail of Death
August 1840	Pokagon band exempted from Potawatomi removal
November 1840	Treaty provides for Miami removal from Indiana
March 1841	William Henry Harrison becomes president of the United States
April 1841	Death of Harrison
August 1841	Death of Miami Chief Richardville, the richest man in Indiana
October 1846	Miami removal from Indiana

1

The Gnadenhutten Massacre (1782)

On March 8, 1782, a militia of white volunteers murdered ninety-six Christian Indians. Twenty-eight men, twenty-nine women, and thirty-nine children were slaughtered. This massacre fueled Indian hatred for white settlers for decades to come.

The seeds of this tragedy were sown ten years before when five Delaware families settled in the Tuscarawas River valley of present-day Ohio. The Indians were led by a white Moravian missionary, David Zeisberger, who had converted them to Christianity. The Christian Indians and missionaries called their village Schoenbrunn. As their numbers increased, they built a church, a school, and sixty log dwellings. They carefully tended their fields and orchards.

Heartened by Schoenbrunn's success, the Moravians built a second mission several miles down the river. They called the new village Gnadenhutten, meaning "Huts of Grace." The leader of Gnadenhutten was an Indian convert named Joshua. He helped Zeisberger deal with neighboring Delaware chiefs. His son, Joshua Jr., played the spinet for church services.

The Moravians were pacifists. They opposed all acts of violence and refused to go to war. When the Revolutionary War began, they urged their Delaware neighbors to remain neutral. However, some Native Americans sided with the British in the fight against the Americans. Shawnee and Wyandot chiefs, for example, quickly sided with the British. One Delaware leader, Captain Pipe, lived among the Wyandot and joined with them in the fight against the Americans. He tried to convince all the Delaware chiefs to fight alongside him.

There was a lot of disagreement among the chiefs on whether to join the war. They were troubled by George Rogers Clark's raids on Shawnee villages to the west. By not taking sides in the conflict, they hoped that their own towns would be spared. In the spring of 1781 American colonel Daniel Brodhead led an attack on Delaware towns in the Tuscarawas valley. As a result, many Delaware moved north to join Captain Pipe. The Long Knives, as the Indians called the Americans, had pushed them into the British camp.

However, the Christian Delaware remained in their villages and maintained their neutrality, welcoming all Indian, American, and British visitors. But despite his pacifist stance, Zeisberger feared an American raid. To build goodwill with the Americans, he warned officials at Fort Pitt of planned Indian attacks by the British allies.

The British were angry that their plans were foiled and accused Zeisberger of treason. In the late summer of 1781 Indian warriors forced his Delaware converts from their villages. The Christian Delaware marched one hundred miles to the Sandusky River to live under the watchful eye of Delaware chief Captain Pipe and the Wyandot. Having no food or supplies for the winter, they soon suffered from hunger and cold.

By February the captives were on the verge of starvation while large supplies of corn lay wasting in their faraway fields. British officials finally allowed them to return home to harvest the corn, and on February 7 a group left for the Tuscarawas valley.

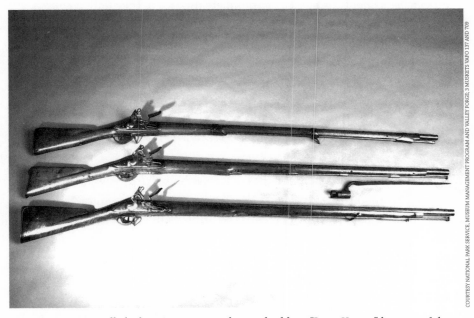

Native Americans called white American settlers and soldiers "Long Knives" because of the long rifles with attached bayonets that they carried. There is a bayonet directly underneath the middle rifle in this photo.

At the same time the British sent out an Indian war party. The warriors attacked the cabin of American settler Robert Wallace. After scalping his wife and baby daughter, the Indians impaled their bodies on trees where a search party would be sure to find them. The warriors then headed for Gnadenhutten, where the Christian Indians were gathering corn. They told of their gruesome deed and warned that a white militia would soon be on their trail. But the Christian Indians did not fear a militia; they had done no wrong.

In Pennsylvania American colonel David Williamson gathered volunteers bent on revenge for the murders of Mrs. Wallace and her daughter. His men approached Gnadenhutten on March 7. They assured the workers in the fields that they meant no harm and offered to take them to Fort Pitt for food and protection. The trusting Indians gratefully accepted the Americans' gesture of friendship and willingly gave up their guns, knives, and axes.

Once the Indians were disarmed, the white men's friendly words turned to shouts and accusations. Someone held up a bloody dress found in one of the village cabins. It was said to belong to the slain Mrs. Wallace. Most likely the dress was left by the guilty warriors in order to implicate the innocent Indians. It is even possible that the British plotted the whole affair to drive the white men to murder, hoping their violence would fire the Indians' lust for revenge.

If it was a British plot, the plan worked perfectly. The sight of the bloody dress whipped the white men into a frenzy. They tied up the Indians and locked them away. Williamson allowed his men to decide their fate. Should the captives be returned to Fort Pitt or put to death? The men stood in a line to vote, and those who favored taking the prisoners to the fort stepped forward. Only eighteen of the ninety men took the step to spare the Indians' lives.

The condemned Christian Delaware spent the night singing and praying. In the morning they were murdered, one by one. The executioners bludgeoned them to death with a large mallet from the cooper's house. They took their scalps as souvenirs. When the massacre was complete, they plundered the village and set fire to the buildings.

Two young boys lived to tell the tale. The first boy had hidden in the cellar of the women's slaughterhouse as blood rained down from the floorboards above. The other boy had been scalped, thrown on a pile, and left for dead. The two boys waited for the men to leave and escaped to the forest.

News of the horrific murders spread through the Indian villages. The Indians vowed a twofold revenge—two white deaths for every Indian death. They increased their raids along the Ohio River and into present-day Kentucky.

Indians murdered settlers and settlers murdered Indians in endless cycles of violence.

In 1798, sixteen years after the massacre, Moravian missionary John Heckewelder returned to Gnadenhutten. In compensation for the grave injustice done by the militia, the American government had set aside three large tracts of land for the Christian Indians. Heckewelder came to prepare it for settlement.

In the years since the massacre, the charred remains of the town had reverted to wilderness. Cutting through the dense overgrowth, Heckewelder found scores of bones on the ground. He piled up the bones and covered them in a mass grave. The mound remains today. It is a haunting reminder of the brutal deaths of innocent Indians at the hands of vengeful white men.

Bones of the victims of the Gnadenhutten Massacre were gathered sixteen years after the massacre and buried in a mass grave. The mound of bones is still visible today.

The Terrible Death of William Crawford

For most of his life William Crawford led a peaceful life as a farmer and surveyor. He became friends with George Washington as a young man. When the American Revolution broke out, Crawford joined Washington. He fought in many of the early eastern battles before being called farther west. In 1781 he participated in Colonel Daniel Brodhead's attack on the Ohio Delaware villages. A British-leaning Delaware chief, Captain Pipe, had led the Indian defense.

Following the Ohio campaign Crawford retired, but he was recalled to service the next year. The British were sending Wyandot and Delaware warriors to attack American settlers. In late May 1782 Crawford led an expedition to destroy Indian villages along the Sandusky River. Unfortunately for Crawford, Colonel David Williamson and men who had perpetrated the Gnadenhutten Massacre were among his volunteers.

Crawford's troops battled the Indians for three days in early June. However, when the British sent reinforcements, Crawford chose to retreat. In the retreat he and a number of his men were captured and brought to Captain Pipe. The Indians tomahawked most of the men immediately, but Crawford suffered a far worse fate.

William Crawford was tortured and burned at the stake in an act of revenge for the Gnadenhutten Massacre.

The Indians sought revenge for the Gnadenhutten Massacre. According to legend, they bound and beat Crawford's naked body, cut off his ears, and shot him from head to toe with charges of gunpowder. They pelted him with burning coals and shoved flaming poles against his charred flesh. It is said they tortured him for two full hours before he finally lost consciousness. In the end they threw him in the fire.

A fellow prisoner, Doctor John Knight, witnessed Crawford's death. In 1783 his account of the event was widely distributed. The story of Crawford's brutal execution inflamed white settlers, just as the Gnadenhutten Massacre had inflamed the Indians.

The killing did not stop when America's war with Britain ended. By 1789 Secretary of War Henry Knox wrote to Washington, "The injuries and murders have been so reciprocal that it would be a point of critical investigation to know on which side they have been the greatest." There was little hope that Indians and white settlers could live together in peace. A full-scale military showdown seemed inevitable.

2

Little Turtle (1752–1812)

I am Meshekinnoquah. The white men call me Little Turtle. I was a Miami warrior.

Long ago my people kindled the first fire at Detroit. The Great Spirit placed the Miami on land whose boundaries stretched from Detroit to the headwaters of the Scioto, down that river to the Ohio, along those waters to the Wabash, and from there to the great lake. Our vast country included what white men know as the Indiana and Michigan Territories, as well as western Ohio.

The Great Spirit was generous. The land met our needs in great abundance. In summer our warriors fished the lakes and streams while our women tended fields of golden corn. Then as leaves dropped from the trees, we moved to winter camps to hunt the wild game. My parents were proud when I brought home my first deer. The story of my victory was told many times around the fire. A Miami man was valued by his deeds in hunting and war.

My father was Aquenochquah. He battled the Iroquois and became a great war chief. Stories of his cunning and bravery were told around many fires. But a son must earn his own honor. To become a man he must fight for his people.

I took my place as a true Miami warrior at the time the Long Knives fought the British. During those years a man of adventure crossed the wide waters from France. His name was Augustin Mottin de La Balme. He came to aid the Long Knives. Like me, he wished to prove himself in battle. He gathered warriors from those who spoke his tongue. He planned to take the British fort at Detroit.

On the way to Detroit his army approached Kekionga, the heart of Miami country. It was the glorious gate through which the words of our chiefs passed from north to south and east to west. It was our greatest center for trade.

One of the wealthiest traders was Charles Beaubien. Though of French blood, Beaubien was a British agent. He supplied our warriors with guns to attack the Long Knives. Beaubien had taken a Miami woman as his wife. Her name was Tacumwah, and she was of my family. We were glad to form a bond with such a rich and powerful man.

When La Balme's men reached Kekionga, our warriors were away on the hunt. The invaders filled their bellies with food and drink from Beaubien's storehouses. For many days they plundered our village. Word of their looting reached my camp. I knew I must avenge the raid and theft of my kinsman's stores. I gathered a war party and waited for the right moment to attack. Finally La Balme's men left Kekionga. Their horses were heavy with stolen goods. After traveling only ten miles they stopped for the night. They camped along the Eel River, a few miles from my home. My warriors surprised them just before dawn. We took more than thirty scalps, including La Balme's. We then returned with our captives to Kekionga. I had earned the respect of my people. Like my father, I would lead them in war.

After the Long Knives defeated the British, more and more white men invaded our land. They came over the mountains and down the streams. They burned the forests and depleted the game. They even murdered our women and children. After hearing of the massacre at Gnadenhutten, we hungered for revenge.

I knew I must defend our land from the white invaders. The Great Spirit had charged the Miami to preserve the forest for our children's children. I fought to fill the white men's hearts with fear so they would retreat and halt their reckless destruction. I led my warriors along the Ohio River and to the settlements beyond. We burned the white men's cabins and stole their horses. With loud cries of victory, we returned to our villages with many scalps and prisoners.

I allowed my people to decide the fate of our captives. First we tested their strength and courage. We burned the weak and cowardly. They were unfit to remain among us. But the strong and brave replaced sons and daughters we had lost through war and disease. We cared for them as our own. One was a boy with hair the color of fire, named William Wells. We called him Apekonit (Wild Carrot). He grew to be a brave Miami warrior, and I gave him my daughter in marriage. Apekonit is my closest partner in serving the needs of our people.

Despite my warriors' daring, the white men continued to ravage our lands. Their numbers increased like flies on a rotting carcass. They demanded of their Father, President George Washington, more ground for their farms. Answering the cries of his people, the president sent a large army to subdue us. The commander of the army was Josiah Harmar.

This depiction of Little Turtle was likely drawn after his death, since Gilbert Stuart's portrait of Little Turtle was destroyed when the British burned Washington, DC, during the War of 1812.

INDIANA HISTORICAL SOCIETY

 In the autumn of 1790 Harmar led 1,500 men to Kekionga. It was the time of the hunt, and few warriors were in our towns. Despite their numbers, the white men could not match our skill and cunning. After sending our women and children to safety, we hid in the surrounding woods and swamps. We waited for a chance to strike back.

When the first Long Knives arrived they found our towns empty. They set fire to our crops and dwellings. Finally they set out to find us. My scouts reported less than two hundred in the search party. I knew my hundred warriors could overcome them easily.

The white men followed the tracks toward my Eel River camp. We dropped trinkets to lure them onward. Our trail of trinkets ended in a clearing surrounded by thick woods and swamp. We would trap them there. We lit a fire and crouched behind the flames. Our trinkets flashed in the firelight. As the white men rushed into the clearing, we fired our muskets. More than sixty fell, few fought back, and most fled. We had defeated the greedy white men. Two days later their army retreated south.

At Kekionga warriors from many tribes joined us. The next day the Long Knives returned to redeem their honor, but we were ready. The rivers ran red with their blood. We had repulsed the white invaders.

Again the settlers demanded their Father's help, so he sent a larger army against us. It was led by General Arthur St. Clair, who gathered more than 2,000 men to destroy our villages. But our scouts were watchful, and we surprised his army at dawn, fifty miles south of Kekionga. We were like foxes pouncing on a flock of roosting chickens.

Before long the ground was littered with hundreds of white bodies. Only twenty-one warriors fell. As the Long Knives fled, I called for the killing to stop. There had been enough blood for one day. I was proud of my warriors. With our Shawnee and Delaware brothers we had turned back the entire American army.

Humiliated by the defeat, Washington searched for a third general to lead his army. He selected General Anthony Wayne, whose army was twice as large as the last. Wayne trained his troops well. He was a chief who never slept. Despite the watchfulness of our scouts, we could not surprise him.

Apekonit left us for the Long Knives. He believed the Indians could not win this war. Reclaiming the name William Wells, he became Wayne's scout. He hoped to gain a position to help our people when the war ended. I was sad to see him go, but we parted as friends. He still had the heart of a Miami warrior.

In time I knew Apekonit had judged correctly. The new American army was too large and well trained for the Indians to attack directly. We could not

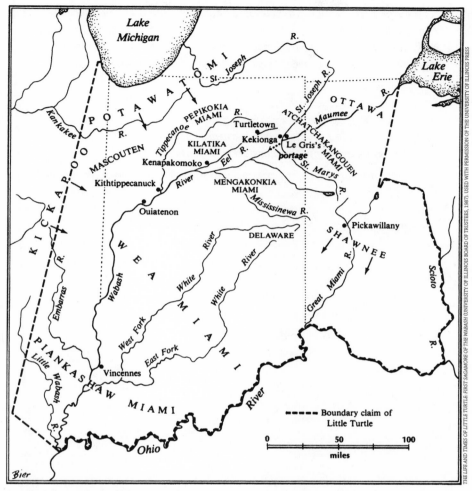

Land of the Miami Indians, ca. 1795.

hope to win such a battle. We could only conquer the Long Knives by cunning.

I ordered my warriors to raid Wayne's supply trains. I hoped that deprived of rations his men would be forced to retreat. But we only slowed their approach. Wayne's army lumbered steadily toward us, raising strong forts on the way.

I asked our British fathers for help. They had long urged us to fight. Though they made many promises, they gave us no cannons. Their words were of little use. Words would not breach the walls of the Long Knives' forts.

As the American army neared our assembly of warriors, Wayne asked once more to discuss peace. I urged my brothers to think carefully on it. Twice we had beaten American armies. Yet twice they had returned, each time with a larger force. We could not always expect good fortune in battle against them.

If we lost a large battle with Wayne, we would negotiate peace as the vanquished. The terms of such a treaty would not favor us. But if we talked with Wayne now, we could speak as victors. Remembering the crushing defeat of St. Clair's army, he would treat us with respect.

In council with chiefs of many tribes, I spoke all I was thinking. My advice was not heeded. I was called a cowardly squaw. The warriors were determined to battle Wayne's army. I had no choice but to accept their decision. I gave my command to Blue Jacket, who spoke strongly for war. With heavy heart I stayed on to fight with my Miami warriors.

We met Wayne in battle near the Maumee River, where a swift storm had toppled a stand of tall trees. Like trees in a whirlwind, our warriors fell before the American army. The British did not rise to help us. They did not leave their fort. Our warriors sought safety within its walls but were turned away. The battle ended quickly, and we were defeated.

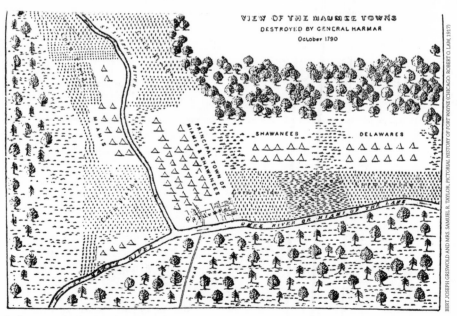

Kekionga, also known as Miami Town, is located in present-day Fort Wayne, Indiana. Kekionga was a hub of Indian life and trade. It was destroyed by General Josiah Harmar's forces in 1790.

Wayne's men cut a trail toward Kekionga, along the banks of the river. On the way they set fire to all our crops and buildings. The sky was black with burning corn. I knew our bellies would growl with hunger that winter.

When Wayne reached Kekionga he raised a new fort. It was called Fort Wayne. Rather than living in the shadow of the American fort, many of my tribesmen moved along the rivers to the west.

The next summer all the tribes traveled to Greenville to bury the tomahawk. I spoke for the Miami. The treaty set a new boundary dividing the Fifteen Fires from Indian lands. The Americans also took sixteen sections within our country for their forts. In return, we would receive a supply of trade goods each year and protection from white squatters.

At the end of our talks Wayne gifted us with silver medals in token of peace. Though we had been defeated, he spoke with respect. He was a brave warrior and a just man. Those are the marks of a great spirit. Though I was the last to sign the treaty, I vowed to be the last to break it.

Since signing the treaty I have made four trips east to meet with American presidents. Each time I have asked them to keep strong drink from entering Indian territory. For the Indians, strong drink is more deadly than war. The drink destroys our warriors' manhood.

On one trip east a doctor gave me strong medicine to protect me from smallpox. This illness has struck down large numbers of our people. Some blame our affliction on witchcraft or the Great Spirit's displeasure. But I do not believe Lalawethika (Tenskwatawa; the Prophet) or other false prophets. I will protect the Miami with the white man's medicine.

During my travels, I have slept in many grand homes. I have dined on fine food and spoken with wise men of many nations. I learned much from them, and they learned from me. Apekonit translated our words. A noted philosopher once asked if I thought the Indians had sprung from the Tartars of Asia. To him I replied, "Why not think that the Tartars descended from us?"

On one of my visits President Washington asked a great artist to draw my likeness. His name was Gilbert Stuart. My painting now hangs in a place of honor with those of other chiefs. The president also presented me with a sword. I treasure his gift as a token of his esteem and friendship. May friendship and peace always unite his people and mine.

~ Little Turtle, 1805

Little Turtle died on July 12, 1812, at the home of his friend and son-in-law, William Wells. His funeral was conducted with full U.S. military honors. He was buried in Wells's orchard with the sword given him by Washington. His burial site was forgotten for many years. Then in 1911, while digging the cellar of a new house, builders discovered the bones of several Indians along with Washington's sword. The grave site is now a small park honoring Little Turtle, the most successful Indian war chief of all time. The plaque reads, "Me-she-kin-no-quah. Chief of the Miami Indians. Teacher of his people. Friend of the United States. His endeavors toward peace should serve as an inspiration for future generations."

Little Turtle's Farm School

Wayne's victory convinced Little Turtle that the tide of white expansion could not be halted by war. After signing the treaty at Fort Greenville, he devoted the rest of his days to maintaining his tribe's friendship with the U.S. government. He believed his tribe's welfare was best served by peace.

As white settlers created new farmland, Indian hunting grounds shrank at an alarming rate. The tribesmen's desire to obtain furs for trade led to over-hunting on their remaining ground. By the early 1800s a shortage of game threatened many tribes with starvation. To secure his tribe's survival, Little Turtle decided the Miami should turn away from hunting and adopt the agricultural techniques of white settlers.

He asked President Thomas Jefferson for plows and farm tools. In the spring of 1804 the Quakers sent a Maryland farmer to Fort Wayne. His name was Philip Dennis, and he was charged with teaching the Miami methods of modern agriculture.

Little Turtle hoped the young Quaker could convince his tribesmen to till the soil. He directed Dennis to a place near the Miami villages, thirty-two miles southwest of Fort Wayne. After the establishment of Wayne's fort, many Miami had left Kekionga to live along the Wabash, Mississinewa, and Eel Rivers. Over the summer Dennis grew bountiful crops. But he was unable to persuade the tribesmen to help. A few would watch him work, but they refused to take up the plow themselves. After bringing in the harvest, Dennis returned to Maryland. He considered his project a failure.

Why did the Miami tribesmen reject Dennis? It is likely their pride made it hard to accept direction from a white man, and Miami crops had always been tended by women and children. They viewed farming as "squaw's work." A man's traditional work was hunting and war. While the Miami mission failed, the Quakers later had some success teaching Black Hoof's Shawnee at Wapakoneta.

While Little Turtle and Black Hoof called for peace with white settlers and adoption of some of their ways, more militant voices were emerging. Tecumseh and his brother, the Prophet, soon urged the Indians to reject white customs and fight for their land. And in time more and more Indians heeded their call.

3

Blue Jacket (1743–1808)

I am known as Blue Jacket, but my Shawnee name is Waweyapiersenwaw, the "Whirlpool." In earlier years I gathered warriors of many fires to fight for our land. Twice I led them to defeat the American army. My success in battle earned the trust of our allies and respect of our enemies. Both the Redcoats and the Long Knives honored me as a great chief.

When the Americans waged war on their British fathers, I joined with the Redcoats. My wife's father was a trader in Detroit and spoke for the British. But it was not only his words that drew me to their side. The Americans were destroying our hunting grounds. With the help of British arms and soldiers we could better defend our land. However, not all tribes took part in the fighting. My old friend, Chief Cornstalk, believed he could keep peace with both the Redcoats and the Long Knives. He was mistaken. When he went to an American post in friendship, he was murdered.

It was clear my decision to join the Redcoats was wise. The Long Knives could not be trusted. They sprang up on our ground like mushrooms in spring. Our warriors needed to stand with our British fathers. Chief Buckongahelas of the Delaware agreed. He built his village near mine and became my closest ally.

In 1778, as leaves fell from the trees, I set out with the Redcoats to retake the American fort at Vincennes. We traveled along the Wabash River, urging the tribes of that region to join us. The British commander was Henry Hamilton. From him I learned the white man's ways of war. Together we captured the fort.

While our warriors were away, the Long Knives burned our crops and villages. They killed our women and children. Seeing their evil deeds, most warriors joined the Redcoats. Many times we crossed the great Ohio River for revenge. We took many scalps and captives. To honor my deeds as a warrior, the British gave me an important paper. It said I was a great man. Despite our victories, the British fathers surrendered to the Long Knives.

They gave them our land. This was a grave injustice. The British had no land to give. The land was always ours.

The white men's treaty meant nothing to me. I continued to raise my tomahawk against the intruders. It is said I hated all white men, but that is not true. My wives were of white blood, and that blood runs through the veins of my children. I only fought to defend our ground.

As a young man I took a white captive as my wife. She was a beautiful squaw with the English name of Margaret Moore. She had lived among us from the age of nine. Together we had a son. When she carried our second child, I allowed her to visit her white family in Virginia. I expected her return, for we had a comfortable home and enjoyed our life together. But after the child was born she stayed to raise her among the white men. As I foresaw, they were not happy there. In later years both she and my daughter came to Ohio to live among the Indians.

My second wife was born of a Shawnee squaw and a French trader. I was pleased to forge bonds with her father. Like him, I was a trader. Through these ties my influence among the Shawnee grew. Like me, they desired the wares of the white man.

My trading business allowed me to provide well for my family. My sons received a fine education in Detroit. I slept on a four-poster bed, and my wife set silver spoons on our table. We had a white captive to keep our cows and make our butter. I treated my servants kindly and saw they were well-fed. They were not eager to leave us.

When we refused to give up our land, the Long Knives again attacked our towns. I moved my village farther west, near Kekionga. Many Miami lived there, and their chiefs welcomed us. Buckongahelas moved his village near mine. From Kekionga I continued to trade our hunters' furs for the goods of British merchants. I also led my warriors along the Ohio River. We stole the white men's horses, burned their cabins, and took their women and children.

During one raid I was captured. The white men threatened to kill me. I told them of my friendship with Daniel Boone. A few years earlier I had taken his son hunting. For this reason they spared my life. That night, when they grew groggy from drink, I escaped. They could not catch me, for I was wise in the ways of the forest. When I finally reached home there was a great celebration. My story was shared around many fires. I had outwitted the Long Knives.

Back home I met with chiefs of many tribes. We talked of saving the land of our ancestors. I spoke as the leader of the Shawnee. I urged all the chiefs to act as one. The American government was sending a large army against us. I knew we could defeat their army with a united Indian force.

The Long Knives marched toward us while many of our men were away at the hunt. They were led by General Josiah Harmar. We emptied our towns of food and directed our women and children to safety. I sent messengers to speed our warriors' return.

After days of looting our deserted villages, the Long Knives withdrew. But lusting for more plunder, they returned. We were ready. Our warriors had come. Many white invaders left their bones on the ground that day. News of our victory spread throughout Indian lands. Warriors from many fires gathered at Kekionga.

Soon a new American army prepared to attack us. This time we would stop the Long Knives before they reached our villages. I led my warriors toward their advancing army. While the Long Knives slept, we painted our faces and readied ourselves for battle. We surprised them at dawn. General Arthur St. Clair's army was no match for our warriors. The scalps we took were beyond counting. The survivors ran from us like frightened squaws. I was honored by both the Shawnee and the Redcoats. I had led a great Indian victory.

In later years Little Turtle tried to steal my success. He claimed the victory. He hoped to increase his prestige with the American government and gain favors for the Miami. His devious son-in-law and friend, William Wells, helped spread his false claim. Little Turtle led his Miami warriors, just as Buckongahelas led the Delaware. But it was I who assembled the entire Indian force. For years after I wore the scarlet-and-gold jacket of a British officer. Little Turtle had no such proof of his standing.

The Long Knives were shamed by their great defeat. They raised another army to send against us. The new army was led by General Anthony Wayne. Again I traveled along the lakes and rivers speaking to warriors of distant fires. They knew of my victory, and I was welcomed among them. I urged all tribes to join in defense of our land. I invited them to come to the place where the Auglaize and Maumee Rivers meet. There I had built my new village. Little Turtle and Buckongahelas built villages near mine. Our new towns were nearer our British friends at Detroit. The British agent, Alexander McKee, kept a large storehouse close by to provide us with food and powder. I commanded more than 2,000 warriors at the Glaize.

Seeing our strength, the Americans sent offers of peace. They even proposed to pay for our land. Our chiefs considered their words. Some spoke for peace, but I knew it was foolish to consent to the Long Knives' demands. We had twice defeated their armies. There was no need to talk with them now. In the summer of 1793 we sent our reply. We refused their money. We suggested they give it to needy white settlers who must remove from our land. We would retreat no farther. When called to the Spirit World we would leave our bones on this ground.

Our British fathers supported us. They built a new fort (Fort Miamis) on the bank of the Maumee River near McKee's storehouse. With their help I knew we would again destroy the American army. As Wayne's Legion marched toward us we prepared to make our stand. We left our villages and moved down the Maumee toward the British fort. I called the chiefs together for our final council of war. Little Turtle spoke for negotiating with the Americans. He said their army had grown too large for us to fight. His words were those of a coward. Once more our warriors chose me to lead them against the Long Knives.

As always, before a great battle we fasted. But Wayne's army did not come, and my warriors grew hungry. The next day many left to hunt for food. It was then that the Long Knives appeared. Their numbers were great. Ours were too few. After emptying our muskets into the flood of Wayne's warriors, we retreated toward Fort Miamis. But when my warriors reached its gates, they were turned away. The Redcoats were false friends. I will never forget their betrayal.

Despite our retreat, many warriors kept their hatchets raised. They waited to battle again, but the Long Knives did not pursue us. As days grew short and our women and children grew hungry, some favored meeting with Wayne. I thought hard upon it. Finally I made my choice. I went to Fort Greenville.

I wore my scarlet jacket and carried my British paper. Wayne could see I was an important chief. I promised to bring the tribes to make the peace the next summer. Wayne promised to give me a paper much finer than my British one.

After the treaty was concluded at Greenville, Wayne kept his promise. He honored me with many gifts. When I asked to meet President George Washington, he granted my request. I traveled to Philadelphia with the most important chiefs while Little Turtle stayed home.

The Americans built me a dwelling near Fort Wayne. It was a fine home, but I decided to move my village near Detroit. There I was a wealthy man. I had plentiful crops and orchards. I brought much meat to our table and fed all who came to my door. I had many friends among the French and Americans, and even the British.

But many tribesmen failed to share my good fortune. They were dying in great numbers. A terrible sickness was sweeping from village to village, cutting a larger swath of death than any army of white men. I knew such devastation could only be wrought by a great power. I wondered at the Great Spirit's wrath. What had our people done to offend? But in my heart I knew. We had surrendered our land.

I soon heard the words of Tenskwatawa (Lalawethika; the Prophet). He was a great prophet and brother of one of my bravest warriors. To Tenskwatawa

Blue Jacket Locked Out of Fort Miamis *is a modern depiction of Blue Jacket attempting to enter the British-held fort. He was turned away, which ultimately led to his surrender and the signing of the Treaty of Greenville.*

the Great Spirit revealed the means of our salvation. He said the Indians must renounce the ways of white men and return to the ways of our ancestors. I knew the Prophet spoke the truth and went to join him.

Tenskwatawa drew many followers. But like all great men he had enemies. One was my old rival. Little Turtle feared the Prophet's power would weaken his own, so he turned the Miami against him. His conspirator, William Wells, spread lies among the white men. He said Tenskwatawa and his brother were preparing for war.

As directed by the Great Spirit, Tenskwatawa established his town near Fort Greenville. Indians from many fires traveled to hear him. The white settlers were alarmed at the large assembly of red men. They feared we would join the British and make war against them. They quickly raised a militia. Before sending their army, their leaders came to weigh our intentions. I spoke for the Prophet and all the Indians at Greenville. I said we desired peace with our white neighbors. We knew the British had dealt with us falsely. We would never join them again to fight the Americans.

I traveled to meet the Ohio governor at Chillicothe. He asked me to address an assembly of citizens. At the given time I entered the courthouse. It was overflowing with white men. I sat beside the governor in a box at the front. Tecumseh was there also with Panther and Roundhead.

Blue Jacket and other Indian chiefs who signed the Treaty of Greenville received medals such as this one to commemorate the event.

I looked out at the large crowd. As I rose the white men grew quiet. I was heartened by the respect they showed me. I offered them words that flowed from my heart. I told them our people were weary of spilling the blood of men, women, and children. We knew the wickedness of war. The Great Spirit was showing us a better way. At Greenville we obeyed the Great Spirit and followed ways of peace.

Later I sat on a porch with my white host. We looked out over the beautiful valley. Tears fell from my eyes. He asked why I wept. I told him, "Sixty years ago I was acquainted with this valley, and no one can now conceive or form the least idea of the torrents of blood that has been shed in this great valley. But all to no purpose. It has done no good, and the very thought of what I have seen and witnessed in this valley makes me weep. It affects my heart and fills it with sorrow. Now I am a very old man, and will soon pass away like all the rest. I desire to live and die in peace!"

~ Blue Jacket, 1807

Blue Jacket addressed the citizens of Chillicothe on September 19, 1807. There is no record of his death, but it is believed that he died near Detroit in early 1808. His life had been filled with great contradictions. Though he worked to unite the Indians, he caused much discord while vying for personal power. This was notably true in respect to his rivalry with Little Turtle.

At the end of his life he supported the Shawnee Prophet, though the Prophet condemned many of the white comforts and customs that Blue Jacket had adopted. Perhaps Blue Jacket sincerely believed in the Prophet's message, or perhaps he saw aligning himself with the Prophet as one last chance to regain the recognition he craved.

Was Blue Jacket a White Man?

Though contrary to fact, a myth identified Blue Jacket as a white man. It was accepted as truth for many years. According to the popular story, Blue Jacket was born to a white frontier family. His name was Marmaduke Van Swearingen. At the age of seventeen "Duke" and his younger brother, Charles, were captured by Indians. Charles was released after Duke agreed to live as an Indian. Duke's captors called him "Blue Jacket" for the blue linsey shirt he wore at the time of his capture. Years later Blue Jacket (Duke) killed Charles while leading his Shawnee warriors against General Arthur St. Clair's army.

It is a fact that Marmaduke Van Swearingen was a real person born in 1763. The fanciful story about him was written by a grandnephew, Thomas Jefferson Larsh. It was published in an Ohio newspaper in 1877. Though unverified, Larsh's story was reprinted in other publications. Over time it was repeated so often that people assumed it was true. The story of a white boy who became an Indian war chief was appealing to Americans. It became the basis of a widely read novel and a play seen by more than a million visitors at an outdoor pageant in Xenia, Ohio.

After twenty-five seasons the pageant closed when historians and scientists concluded Marmaduke and Blue Jacket were not the same person. Records show that Blue Jacket fought in Lord Dunmore's War in 1774 when Marmaduke was only eleven years old. And there is no known historical account in which Blue Jacket's contemporaries refer to him as a white man.

Finally in 2006 DNA testing on the descendants of Marmaduke Van Swearingen and Blue Jacket showed no relationship between the two families. The Blue Jacket myth was finally laid to rest. But Blue Jacket's true story is just as intriguing. It tells of a courageous, though vain, Shawnee warrior who fought and befriended white men. Though he married white women, he supported an Indian prophet who denounced the practice. The life of the real Blue Jacket reflects many of the conflicts the Indians faced with the onslaught of white civilization.

4

St. Clair's Defeat (1791)

After the Indians repelled Josiah Harmar's troops in 1790, the new American government was frustrated. Settlers demanded protection from Indians who were attacking their flatboats and cabins. Once again President George Washington ordered a strike against Kekionga, the heart of Indian resistance. He selected General Arthur St. Clair to lead the army and directed him to march north from Fort Washington, at present-day Cincinnati, and build a string of forts along the way. Then, on November 4, 1791, Miami Chief Little Turtle led an attack on the U.S. Army. The resulting Indian victory was the worst defeat of the American army in the history of the United States. To white Americans it became known as St. Clair's Defeat.

St. Clair was governor of the Northwest Territory and had served admirably in the American Revolution. But by 1791 he was not suited to lead an army. Severely afflicted with gout, he was unable to mount a horse without pain, and his men often carried him on a litter.

The infirm general commanded a ragtag army. Only one in ten of his men had military experience. Many recruits had been pulled from jails and saloons. Though his Kentucky militiamen were experienced Indian fighters, they lacked military discipline and refused to obey orders. A large group of women and children followed the army, which severely disrupted camp life.

When the campaign began, Washington advised St. Clair, "Beware of surprise . . . when you halt for the night be sure to fortify your camp—and again and again, General, beware of surprise!" Though long on advice, the government was short on support. An officer described the army as "badly clothed, badly paid and badly fed." Widespread corruption among suppliers resulted in shoddy equipment. Cheaply made tents and clothing offered little protection from the cold, wet weather. The poor-grade powder barely ignited. The weary

MAJ. GEN. ARTHUR ST CLAIR.

Arthur St. Clair was the governor of the Northwest Territory from 1787 to 1800. In 1791 General St. Clair's army experienced a crushing defeat by the forces of Little Turtle and Blue Jacket. This battle became known as St. Clair's Defeat.

troops had to chop their way through dense woods with warped ax blades.

Progress was extremely slow. On September 11, 1791, the army established its first new fort, Fort Hamilton. A month and only forty miles later, it erected Fort Jefferson. By then food had become so scarce that the men were put on half rations and the horses were dying. At Kekionga Little Turtle's scouts informed him of all the Long Knives' problems.

On October 24 St. Clair continued toward Kekionga. He advanced only six miles to the site of present-day Greenville, Ohio. There his men camped in sleet and snow, waiting for food and supplies. On October 30 they inched ahead seven more miles. But the next day St. Clair received disturbing news. He was told that half the militia had deserted.

Immediately St. Clair ordered his most experienced unit, the First American Regiment, to pursue the deserters. By the time he learned only sixty men had fled, the damage was done. He had sent his best-trained troops away. Desertion, disease, and the need to man the new forts had depleted his army.

While Little Turtle's scouts kept him well-informed, St. Clair received little news about the Indians. He did not know that more than 1,000 warriors had gathered at Kekionga. Mingo, Cherokee, Wyandot, Potawatomi, Ojibwa, and Ottawa braves had joined the Miami, Shawnee, and Delaware warriors. Little Turtle knew the American army was weak. He conferred with Shawnee Chief Blue Jacket and Delaware Chief Buckongahelas. Instead of waiting at Kekionga, the three great war chiefs chose to move southward to surprise the Long Knives with a dawn attack.

On November 3 the American troops made camp by the banks of a stream. St. Clair believed it was the St. Marys River, fifteen miles south of Kekionga. Actually it was the Wabash River, fifty miles short of his goal. Woods and swamp surrounded the campsite. It was not large enough to hold the entire army, so the Kentucky militia crossed the water.

St. Clair's men suffered from cold, hunger, and fatigue. Ignoring Washington's advice to "beware of surprise," St. Clair did not order his weary men to dig trenches or build earthworks before retiring for the night. He had no idea the Indians were just a few miles away. That night an American patrol spotted warriors, but St. Clair was not wakened to hear its report. The general and his army slept while the Indians prepared for battle.

The warriors rose early and crept through the woods before dawn. They moved in a crescent formation, spilling around the American camp. St. Clair's soldiers ate breakfast, unaware of the surrounding danger.

Just before 6:00 a.m. shots rang out, followed by deafening war cries. The frightened Kentuckians threw down their weapons and plunged through the icy water to the main camp. Their hasty flight broke the lines of troops moving into fighting formation. Amidst the confusion and cover of smoke, Indian warriors burst into the camp.

There was widespread panic among the women, children, and new recruits. Calmly the Indians carried out Little Turtle's plan. They first targeted the army's officers and artillery. Little Turtle's son-in-law, William Wells (Apekonit), led his Miami sharpshooters in shooting them one by one. The strategy worked brilliantly. Deprived of leadership and cannon fire, the camp's defenses quickly crumbled. In three hours the ground was littered with white bodies.

Despite heavy casualties among his officers, St. Clair survived the attack. His gout saved him. He was unable to don his dress uniform and had worn a plain coat and hat, which hid his identity from the Miami marksmen.

St. Clair saw that the battle was lost and ordered a retreat. In a desperate charge, his men broke through the Indian lines to the road back to Fort Jefferson. They fled pell-mell, discarding guns and equipment along the way. Those unable to run were trampled by their comrades. The jubilant Indians soon gave up the chase and returned to the battlefield. They butchered the wounded and collected the spoils of war—eight cannons and twelve hundred muskets.

Following the battle, St. Clair reported 881 casualties, two-thirds of the American army. Only twenty-one Indians died. It was a crushing blow for the young nation. Washington demanded St. Clair's resignation.

The Indians had decisively defeated the Long Knives. Yet they had not yet won the larger war. White settlers continued to clamor for Indian land. And a larger and stronger American army eventually faced the Indians.

Fort Recovery

The American government was determined to open the land north of the Ohio River for safe white settlement. After St. Clair's defeat Congress increased the army's funding. Washington named another new commander, General Anthony Wayne. Washington hoped Wayne could achieve what Harmar and St. Clair had failed to do. He charged Wayne with forcing the Indians to submit to the will of the American government.

Wayne called his army "The Legion of the United States." In June 1792 he began training his troops near Pittsburgh. He drilled them thoroughly and methodically. He was a harsh taskmaster. For example, a man with a dirty uniform got twenty lashes, and a soldier found sleeping on duty suffered a hundred.

While Wayne trained his troops, Shawnee chief Blue Jacket traveled far and wide, from the upper Great Lakes to the Mississippi River, urging all tribes to join in defending the land north of the Ohio River. His call for Indian solidarity was enhanced by the recent victory over St. Clair's army. In September 1792 chiefs of many tribes gathered along the Maumee and Auglaize Rivers in present-day northwest Ohio, an area known as the Glaize. They agreed to stand united on the demand for the Ohio River boundary. They refused to allow American settlement north of the river.

In May 1793 Wayne brought 2,600 well-trained and disciplined troops to Fort Washington near Cincinnati. Meanwhile, two thousand warriors gathered two hundred miles north at the Glaize. Peace talks between the tribes and the U.S. government failed. Without agreement over the boundary issue, war was inevitable.

In October Wayne's Legion advanced to Fort Jefferson. Unable to protect a long supply line from attack, Wayne built another fort only six miles beyond Fort Jefferson. He named it Fort Greenville in honor of his Revolutionary War comrade, Nathaniel Greene.

In December Wayne decided to build a fort at the site of St. Clair's defeat, twenty-three miles northwest of Fort Greenville. From this position he could launch an attack on the Indian stronghold farther north. Eight companies of infantry and a detachment of artillery arrived at the scarred battle site on Christmas Day 1793. There they found thousands of bones scattered across the ground and buried more than six hundred skulls before raising the fort.

The soldiers secured the fort well, clearing the ground for a thousand feet around its stockade. With the help of William Wells, they located and mounted three cannons, which had been buried by the Indians after St. Clair's battle. The new fort was named Fort Recovery to celebrate reclaiming the ground from the Indians.

Once more the Indians prepared to fight a large American army. Returning from their winter hunt, more than a thousand warriors reassembled near the Maumee rapids. They were heartened by signs of support from the British. The governor of Canada, Lord Dorchester (Sir Guy Carleton), ordered a post built nearby. It was named Fort Miamis.

The Indian leaders knew the American forts were nearly impenetrable. However, despite strong forts and a large number of well-trained troops,

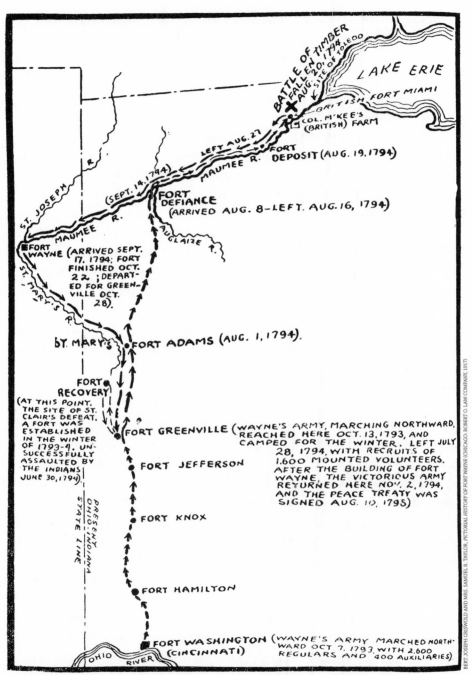

A map illustrating General Anthony Wayne's campaign to subdue the Indians, 1793–95. Wayne established Fort Wayne on the location once occupied by Kekionga.

Wayne's Legion did have a weakness. The troops could not adequately defend their supply lines, which stretched many miles through the wilderness. Little Turtle and Blue Jacket plotted to cut off Wayne's supplies. They hoped that a shortage of food and gunpowder would force Wayne to retreat. On June 19 the Indian warriors began marching south.

On June 28 the Indians came to the road linking Fort Recovery and Fort Greenville. Shawnee, Miami, and Wyandot leaders favored continuing on to cut the supply line south of Greenville, where Wayne kept most of his troops. Without delivery of food, Wayne would be forced to abandon his headquarters at Fort Greenville as well as Fort Recovery. However, a supply train was entering Fort Recovery. If the Indians attacked the train when it left the fort the next day, they could easily take many supplies. Despite Little Turtle and Blue Jacket's determination to continue south, they could not dissuade the Potawatomi, Ottawa, and Ojibwa warriors from striking the nearby, easy mark.

The next morning the American convoy left Fort Recovery to return to Fort Greenville. Fifty men on horseback and ninety riflemen escorted 360 packhorses. Within earshot of the small fort the Indians ambushed them, and within fifteen minutes they captured three hundred horses and killed or wounded fifteen white men. The warriors were elated with their success. Instead of withdrawing to strike the supply line farther south, they attacked the fort.

Only 250 men defended Fort Recovery, but the Indians had to cross a thousand feet of open ground to reach it. Gun and cannon fire from the fort kept them at bay. When darkness finally fell, the Indians tried to recover their dead by torchlight. The next morning the warriors resumed their siege, despite urging from British officers to retreat. By the afternoon they realized their efforts were futile. Forty warriors lay dead, and twenty more were wounded. The losses were large by Indian standards. However, the greater toll was to their unity. The Shawnee, Miami, and Wyandot blamed the Potawatomi, Ottawa, and Ojibwa warriors for their reckless assault on the fort. The Potawatomi, Ottawa, and Ojibwa accused the others of cowardice and packed up their plunder and headed for home. Indian unity had splintered.

Estimates of the number of Indians involved in the attack range from several hundred to two thousand. Regardless of the exact numbers, it is certain that the fight was waged at the height of the Indian confederacy. The Battle of Fort Recovery was a major turning point in the conflict between the Indians and the Americans. Never again would such a large native force unite to confront American expansion.

5

Wayne's Victory (1794)

By the Maumee River a tornado once felled a mighty stand of trees. Years later the Indians made their stand against the American army at this spot, hoping that the fallen timbers would provide cover from General Anthony Wayne's advancing troops. At Fallen Timbers they hoped to turn back the tide of white expansion.

After their failure to take Fort Recovery, the tribes at the heart of the Indian confederacy returned to the Glaize, near present-day Defiance, Ohio. It had become their main stronghold after defeating General Arthur St. Clair's army. Shawnee chief Blue Jacket, Miami chief Little Turtle, and Delaware chief Buckongahelas had flourishing villages there. It was also home to French and British traders.

Smarting from the setback at Fort Recovery, Little Turtle went to Detroit to determine how much help the Indians could expect from the British. He feared the Indians alone could not defeat Wayne's army. He asked for men and cannon but received only vague assurances. This confirmed his growing belief that the Indians should broker peace with the Americans.

In early August 1794 news came that Wayne's army was moving along the Auglaize River toward the Indian towns. The Indians quickly deserted their villages, leaving most of their belongings behind. The warriors retreated down the Maumee River to the rapids near British Fort Miamis. The women and children traveled to safety beyond the fort, near the shores of Lake Erie.

Wayne arrived at the Glaize on August 8. Well-tended gardens and endless fields of corn surrounded his troops. Wayne defied the Indians by claiming the heart of their territory. He began building a fort at the confluence of the Maumee and Auglaize Rivers. The fort was aptly named Fort Defiance.

ELIZABETH O'MALEY

Fort Recovery was built by General Anthony Wayne in 1793 in response to St. Clair's Defeat. Part of the fort has been re-created and is operated by the Ohio Historical Society and Fort Recovery Historical Society.

On August 14 Wayne sent out his last offer to negotiate peace. The Indians stalled for time, replying that their chiefs needed to gather to discuss his proposal. Taking no chances, Wayne pressed forward. He established Camp Deposit, within eight miles of the British fort.

There was heated debate as the chiefs held their council. Some argued for attacking Wayne's camp, just as they had stormed St. Clair's. Others favored a defensive stance, as when they had turned back General Josiah Harmar. Little Turtle spoke for ending the fight altogether and negotiating with Wayne. He believed the American army had become too large and powerful for the Indians to defeat without more aid from the British. Blue Jacket disagreed vehemently and labeled Little Turtle a coward.

The chiefs decided in favor of Blue Jacket. Little Turtle accepted the decision and stayed to lead his Miami warriors against the Americans. Overall command of the battle was given to Blue Jacket. On August 18 the Indians formed a defensive line two miles south of Fort Miamis. They waited in the thick woods, expecting Wayne's army to advance toward the fort the next day. As was their custom before battle, they fasted.

William Wells, however, knew the Indian custom. He advised Wayne to delay his attack until the warriors were weak with hunger. By August 20 many of the Indians had left to find food. Wayne seized the advantage and moved forward. Mounted volunteers attacked the Indians hiding behind the trees and high grass. The Indians fought fiercely, forcing a brief American retreat. Then Wayne ordered his men to charge with bayonets and roust them from cover. Reluctantly, the Indians gave up their ground. They fired their muskets, retreated, reloaded, and fired and retreated again.

In the midst of the battle were two Shawnee brothers who revived the conflict years later. The first, Tecumseh, led his party of warriors at the center of the Indian line. The other, Lalawethika or Tenskwatawa (the Prophet), retreated to the sidelines. Also in the battle was William Henry Harrison, who served as an aide to Wayne. Harrison became the Shawnee brothers' greatest adversary.

The full fury of Wayne's army hit the Indians like a giant whirlwind. Many warriors fell, and within ninety minutes the rest fled toward Fort Miamis. The warriors pressed against the gates of the British fort, seeking protection, But the commander of the fort, Major William Campbell, refused them entry. The Indians were forced to continue their desperate flight. This betrayal by the British was a blow to the Indians' spirit that they would never forget.

By most accounts the Indians were far outnumbered. The one prisoner taken by the Americans, trader Antoine Lasselle, reported only 900 Indians faced Wayne's 3,000 troops. British agent Alexander McKee, who participated in the fighting, claimed there were only 400 Indians.

Regardless of their true numbers, the Indians were quickly routed. Estimates of casualties vary, but there were no more than thirty American deaths. At the time the enormity of the victory was not fully realized by the men of Wayne's force. They expected a larger battle ahead. They did not know Indian resistance had collapsed and the war was won.

Wayne himself tended to exaggerate the dimensions of the fight. He claimed his army had overcome "two thousand Indians and the whole Detroit militia." Camping boldly within view of the British fort, he traded insults with its commander. Meanwhile, his men ate from the garrison's garden and set fire to its outbuildings. Campbell seethed at Wayne's arrogance but put forth no resistance. Campbell and Wayne feared an outright fight would provoke war between their two nations.

After two days of taunting the British, Wayne returned to Camp Deposit, and then to Fort Defiance. He pursued a scorched-earth policy. Thousands of acres of Indian corn and vegetables, homes, tools, and furnishings were turned to ashes. After three weeks at Fort Defiance, Wayne cut a road for forty-eight miles along the Maumee River to the old Miami stronghold, Kekionga.

There his men built a new fort, naming it Fort Wayne. Wayne had accomplished what Harmar and St. Clair had failed to do. The new fort established American authority deep within Indian territory.

Agents of the British: Simon Girty, Alexander McKee, and Matthew Elliott

At the time of the American Revolution, three frontiersmen defected from the American side. They were Simon Girty, Alexander McKee, and Matthew Elliott. The three fled Fort Pitt to offer their services to the British at Detroit. For many years they worked as agents of the British and encouraged the Indians' struggle against American expansion.

Earlier, in 1755, an army of French soldiers and Indian warriors captured Girty, and the Seneca tribe adopted him. Before his return to white society he learned several Indian languages. When the Revolution began, Girty sided with the Americans. He served as an Indian agent, spy, and interpreter. In February 1778 he accompanied General Edward Hand on an expedition to seize British supplies believed hidden at an Indian village in present-day Ohio. Failing to find them, the troops slaughtered a group of Delaware women and children. The next month Girty defected to the British.

For many years Girty was the most hated man on the American frontier. Settlers blamed him for instigating Indian raids. They also held him responsible for the torture and burning of William Crawford. It was widely believed that Girty refused Crawford's cries for mercy and reveled in his agony. In truth, there was little he could have done to dull the warriors' desire to avenge the Gnadenhutten Massacre (see Chapter 1).

Girty fought alongside the Indians at many crucial battles, including St. Clair's defeat and the Battle of Fallen Timbers. Following the American victory Girty moved across the Detroit River to Canada. From there he continued to serve the British Indian Department. His notoriety as a frontier villain endured. During the War of 1812 Americans put a price on his head, and the Canadians hid him from invading American troops.

Another famous British agent was McKee, who was the son of an Irish trader and a Shawnee woman. Becoming a trader himself, he moved easily within both cultures. After fleeing to Detroit with Girty and Elliott, he became an interpreter in the British army.

General "Mad" Anthony Wayne.

Along with the Indian chief, Blue Jacket, McKee accompanied Colonel Henry Hamilton on his capture of the American fort of Vincennes. Throughout the next three decades McKee maintained close ties with the Shawnee leader. From his post at the Maumee Rapids he supplied Indian warriors with guns to battle the Long Knives.

The assembly of warriors waiting to confront Wayne's army in 1794 was as much McKee's creation as Blue Jacket's. McKee was also central to negotiations between the tribes and the American government. He advised the Indians to insist on the Ohio River as the boundary of white settlement. This matched Britain's goal of keeping an Indian buffer zone between British and American territory.

Following the Indians' defeat at Fallen Timbers, McKee settled in Canada, where he died in 1799. Following his death, the third of the three Fort Pitt renegades, Elliott, took charge of British Indian affairs. Like Girty and McKee, Elliott was well-regarded by the tribes of the Northwest Territory.

Elliott came from Ireland as a young man. At the outbreak of the Revolutionary War he was a trader in the Ohio country and supported the American cause. But when American militia destroyed Indian towns, he became disillusioned and joined the British. In 1782 he led the Indians to defeat William Crawford's troops in their Sandusky expedition.

After the Revolution Elliott worked closely with McKee to rally the Indians to fight the Long Knives. Though the Indians were defeated at Fallen Timbers, Elliott continued his efforts to keep them allied with the British. As Superintendent of Indian Affairs he supplied food and guns to Tecumseh and his warriors. By the War of 1812 Elliott was well into his seventies. Despite his age, he fought beside the Indians at the siege of Fort Meigs and the Battle of the Thames.

Elliott died during a short illness in 1814. Soon after, the United States and Britain signed a treaty of peace. The Indians of the Old Northwest had lost their final battle against white expansion, and their long alliance with the British against the United States ended.

6

William Wells (1770–1812)

My English name is William Wells. The Miami call me Apekonit, which means "Wild Carrot." It is said I was named this for my red hair, but wild carrots do not match my hair. I was actually named for my large appetite. When my captors brought me to their Eel River village, I was hungry as a bear in springtime. The women laughed as I gobbled down bowl after bowl of their wild carrot soup.

I was fourteen then and not yet a man. The day of my capture I had gone hunting with three of my friends. I loved to hunt and was an excellent marksman. Nothing brought me more pleasure than roaming the forest, finding adventure behind every tree.

At the time of my capture I was living with William Pope at Louisville. He was my father's friend. They had fought Indians together until the savages killed my father. Since my mother was also dead, I was sent to live with Pope.

When the Indians jumped from the shadows, I showed no fear. As we made our way north I planned the story I would tell my brothers on my return. I was sure I would escape. But the farther we went, the more I felt the hollow in my belly and worried about finding my way back home.

Many days passed. I was half-starved when we reached the Eel River village, where I was forced to run the gauntlet. The Indians formed two long lines. As I raced through the tunnel between them, they hurled rocks and struck me with switches. This was a test of my courage, and I was deter-mined to pass it. Despite the pain I looked straight ahead without crying.

I was rewarded for my bravery. The women filled me with carrot soup and smeared my wounds with bear grease. I was grateful for their kindness. With my stomach full I started once more to enjoy my adventure. Soon I was adopted by the village chief and lost my desire for home. I was so busy learning Indian ways that I seldom thought of my white friends and family.

My new father was Gaviahatte, which means "the Porcupine." He taught me the skills of a warrior. My new life as an Indian suited my boyish heart. What boy would not prefer the forest to the classroom? I quickly earned the respect of the men and boys for my feats as a hunter.

I was proud to join Miami warriors on their raids along the Ohio River. I would call out to the flatboats for help. My white skin lured them close to shore. Then the warriors would mount their deadly attack. We returned many scalps to the Eel River villages. Some say I betrayed my own people. But at that time Gaviahatte was my father, and his tribe, my family. My people were the Indians.

I had learned of the massacre at Gnadenhutten (see Chapter 1). I had heard how white men burned Indian villages and took Indian land as their own. Like most boys, I had a simple desire for justice and a thirst for the praise of my peers. And as I grew into a man, I craved the challenge of battle. I was proud to fight for the Miami.

Eventually my white brothers found me and took me back to Kentucky. My white brother, Sam, had done quite well in life, and his house had every manner of comfort. But after a few days sleeping on linen and eating my fill at his table, I grew restless. I escaped and hurried home to marry an Indian girl.

By then the government was sending large armies against the Indians. I thought the Americans were no match for our warriors. Our leader was Little Turtle, the most cunning war chief of all. I had come to his notice on our raids along the river. He treated me as a son, and in time he became my closest friend.

In August 1791 I went to Kekionga with Gaviahatte to arm for battle. We knew General Arthur St. Clair was training his troops at Fort Washington. Little Turtle expected him to march on Kekionga before winter. We prepared to defend our land from the Long Knives.

While we were away at Kekionga, five hundred Kentucky militiamen attacked our Eel River village. They murdered women and children, took thirty-four prisoners, and burned our dwellings and crops to the ground. When I learned my wife and my mother were captured, I went to war with hatred in my heart. I wanted to wreak revenge on those who had stolen my family.

On November 5, 1791, we surprised the American army at dawn. Little Turtle directed our attack. I was proud to lead his sharpshooters. We moved directly in front of the cannons. My braves picked off the artillerymen and silenced their weapons. Without firepower the Americans had no chance against us.

JACOB PIATT DUNN, TRUE INDIAN STORIES (INDIANAPOLIS: SENTINEL PRINTING COMPANY, 1908)

Captain William Wells from a medallion portrait owned by his family in 1908.

Within three hours hundreds of white men were dead. Their comrades fled in panic. We followed for a short while but then turned back; the battle had been won. With swift blows of the tomahawk we dispatched the wounded to their maker. In the delirium of victory I was immune to the white men's agony. After burying the cannons, we left with all the scalps and loot we could carry.

In the spring I went with my father to the post at Vincennes to request the release of prisoners. I sorely missed my wife and my mother. Hearing of my whereabouts, Sam came to the fort. Again he pressed me to go with him to

Louisville. I was not inclined toward his invitation but agreed, hoping he could help gain my family's freedom.

With my brother I waited for General Rufus Putnam, who had been sent to negotiate peace with the Indians. For many days and nights Sam and I shared our stories. Our kinship was revived. When I learned that he had served in St. Clair's army, it weighed heavy in my heart that I might have killed my own brother.

In July I finally met Putnam. Hoping to earn my family's release, I offered to be his interpreter. I was fluent in the Miami language and familiar with the speech of many neighboring tribes. He gave me the job for a dollar a day. But more important, he released my wife and mother. I had learned an important lesson. I could best care for my Miami family as a white man. From that day on I worked for the Americans.

When I returned to Kekionga I told Little Turtle my thoughts. Settlers were flooding the Ohio Valley. Though the Indians had defeated St. Clair, they could not stand forever against the growing American force. In the end the Long Knives would take what they wanted.

I joined General Anthony Wayne's Legion as a scout. Some say the information I brought him caused the Indians' defeat. But the army was large and well-trained. Wayne was a brilliant war chief, perhaps the equal of Little Turtle. In time he would beat back the Indians, with or without my help.

After peace was made at Greenville, I worked hard to preserve it. I knew that peace was best for the Indians. War would only further shrink their numbers. I became Little Turtle's interpreter, and later, Indian agent at Fort Wayne. I helped him obtain generous provisions for the Miami. I hoped the annuities would sustain them until they learned the white man's more prosperous ways.

Little Turtle was partner in all my endeavors. He gave me his daughter, Sweet Breeze, in marriage, connecting us as kin as well as friends. I built Sweet Breeze a home near the fort where we cared for a son and three daughters. My fields and orchards kept food on our table and supplied the needs of the fort. Little Turtle spent much time at our home when not at his Eel River village. I was not a rich man but made a good life for my family.

Unfortunately our days of peace and good fortune were numbered. Sweet Breeze succumbed to illness in the winter of 1805. At the same time Lalawethika (Tenskwatawa), the Shawnee Prophet, was arousing the Indians' warlike passions. I tried to warn the governor of his mischief, but he preferred to turn a deaf ear.

My daughters sorely missed the care of their mother and deserved more comfort than my situation allowed. After consulting with Little Turtle, I sent them to Sam in Kentucky. There they received a good education and learned to enjoy the refinements of white culture. The life of an Indian might suit a young man well, but with age I came to appreciate the benefits of white society.

As the years passed, my duties as Indian agent grew more and more difficult. I continued to distribute annuities and to hold council meetings with the chiefs. However, my most important job was maintaining good relations with the tribes. But that became an impossible task.

The government was determined to acquire more Indian land. Despite the promises made at Greenville, new boundaries were drawn. Again and again new treaties were signed. As might be expected, Indian resentment grew as their holdings dwindled.

The governor of the Indiana Territory, William Henry Harrison, blamed me for stirring the tribes' unrest. But it was his dealings that caused the trouble. He brokered treaties that took millions of acres from the tribes. It was little wonder that many tribesmen turned from Little Turtle and assumed the hostile attitude of the Prophet and his brother, Tecumseh. I warned the secretary of war about the threat the brothers posed, but like the governor he turned a deaf ear to my warnings.

To make matters worse, the old Shawnee, Blue Jacket, joined the brothers' cause. The old man spoke with the Ohio governor and tried to poison his

This document, signed by William Wells, states, "I promise for what has been received and for what I may receive to promote to the extent of my power the interest of the United States with the northwestern Indians." With loyalties to both the United States and to the Miami tribe, Wells was sometimes accused of favoring the Indians at the expense of the government.

mind against me. He had always been jealous of Little Turtle and anxious to raise his own standing. His alliance with the Shawnee brothers was further proof of their evil intent. Blue Jacket had always favored war.

As I feared, Indian violence became more frequent. Some said war was inevitable, but I view my inability to keep the peace as my greatest failure. My children carried both Indian and white blood in their veins. Living in the space between two worlds, I had always hoped to join them together.

Little Turtle passed to the Spirit World in July 1812. I mourned his loss as a son mourns the death of a father. War will reach us soon, and without his presence the Indians will surely join hands with the British. There is little I can do to dissuade them.

I have a new wife, a white woman. We have one child and another on the way. The time has come to look after my family and make my home in Kentucky. The governor knows I desire to leave my post but implores me to stay at Fort Wayne.

Already white citizens have moved inside the fort. They have good reason to fear, for the danger is great. Harrison believes that only I can quell the rage of the Indians gathered around the stockade. It is difficult to know where my greater duty lies, but ultimately, I must think of my family. I must take them to safety.

Today I learned that General William Hull has ordered the evacuation of Fort Dearborn. He fears it will soon be stormed by Indian warriors, as was Michilimackinac to the north. The fort's commander is Nathan Heald, husband of my niece, Rebecca. She is with him now and in immediate danger.

I feel I must go to Heald's aid. I will gather Miami warriors to go with me. Hopefully we will arrive in time to bring the women and children to Fort Wayne. Then I will take Rebecca to Kentucky along with my wife and children. Once my family is safe, I will do all in my power to restore peace with the Indians.

~ William Wells, 1812

With thirty Miami warriors, Wells hurried to Fort Dearborn on August 14, 1812, at present-day Chicago, 160 miles northwest of Fort Wayne. He found the situation dire. Despite their promises of safe passage, it was clear that the hundreds of Potawatomi surrounding the fort were in league with the British.

Before escorting the residents from the fort, Wells blackened his face. This was the custom of a Miami warrior preparing for death or battle. With his warriors he took his place at the head of the slow-moving caravan. The soldiers followed and then the wagons of women and children. They traveled along the shore of Lake Michigan between the dunes and the water.

Suddenly bullets began to fly. Waves of Potawatomi warriors rose from behind the sand hills, outnumbering the white men ten to one. They charged toward the wagons. Wells rushed to the rear to protect them. He died on August 15, 1812, defending the women and children.

The Potawatomi warriors cut out his heart and ate it. Though a horrific act, it was a sign of respect. They believed that by eating his heart they would absorb his daring and courage.

Of the sixty-six men, nine women, and eighteen children who evacuated the fort, thirty-eight men, two women, and twelve children were killed. The rest were captured and sold to the British. Most of the captives, including Rebecca and Nathan Heald, were eventually set free and returned home. The role of Wells's Miami warriors is uncertain. Some say they fought with Wells, and others say they abandoned him. Harrison accused them of joining the Potawatomi in the massacre.

As he hoped, Wells's children were all well educated. His son, William Wayne Wells, graduated from West Point. Mary Wells, the youngest daughter of William and Sweet Breeze, married Judge James Wolcott, a prosperous businessman and mayor of Maumee, Ohio. The Wolcotts' beautiful home was not far from the site of the Battle of Fallen Timbers. Mary was known for her generous hospitality to both Indians and white settlers and served as a bridge between the two cultures.

James Logan

In August 1812, after Wells's departure for Fort Dearborn, anger surged among the Indians pressing around Fort Wayne. It was decided to move the women and children to safety in Ohio. James Logan, a Shawnee Indian, was entrusted with this mission. Logan guided the group through a hundred miles of swamp and wilderness to Piqua, Ohio. He was so devoted to his duty that he stayed awake the entire journey.

William Wells's family was in the party escorted by Logan. Like Wells, Logan had been captured during the border wars of the 1780s. General Benjamin Logan seized the young Indian boy, Spemica Lawba (High Horn), during his raids on the Shawnee villages. General Logan and his men had attacked the boy's village while most of the warriors were away. They took many prisoners, including twelve-year-old Spemica Lawba. Like Tecumseh, a future Shawnee leader, Spemica Lawba had just witnessed the death of Moluntha, the peace-seeking Shawnee leader (see Chapter 10). The general was so impressed by the young boy's spirit that he took him home to Kentucky. Spemica Lawba became James Logan. He learned English and was taught to read and write alongside the Logan children.

In a few years James Logan was traded for a white captive during an exchange of prisoners. It is likely that Logan was glad to return to his tribe. But a prisoner exchange was often flooded with tears. Some Indians had grown to prefer the comforts of white society, and many white boys preferred the freer Indian life. Young children, white and Indian, often clung to their adoptive mothers, the only mothers they knew. Though Logan returned to the Shawnee, he kept his English name and maintained his friendship with the Logans. He became influential in his tribe and served as an interpreter.

Logan took the women and children from Fort Wayne just in time. By late August the fort was surrounded by hundreds of hostile warriors. Logan and two of his Shawnee friends, Bright Horn and Captain Johnny, volunteered to carry messages in and out of the fort. It was an extremely dangerous duty. Having shown their loyalty and courage, the three became scouts for William Henry Harrison, governor of the Indiana Territory.

Harrison sent them to scout the area of the Maumee rapids near the British Fort Miamis. While on this mission they came upon a large group of Indians allied with the British and were forced to fall back to the American camp. A Kentucky officer accused Logan of giving intelligence to enemy Indians. Logan was deeply insulted by the charge.

The next morning Logan again headed down the Maumee with his two companions. He was determined to return with proof of his loyalty. While stopping to rest, the three were surprised by seven of the enemy, led by Potawatomi chief Winnemac.

Logan quickly devised a plan of escape. He convinced Winnemac that his group was leaving the Americans to join the British. Winnemac returned their weapons. Then Logan and his friends turned them on their captors. They killed two warriors and fatally wounded another. The remaining four escaped but not before lodging bullets in Logan and Bright Horn.

Captain Johnny took Winnemac's scalp and lashed his wounded comrades to the enemies' horses. They reached the American line the next morning. News of the episode spread through the camp. Logan's loyalty was vindicated. When he died a few days later he was buried with full military honors. Like Logan, many Indians fought for the United States during the War of 1812. Unfortunately, their loyalty was often questioned, and their villages burned along with those of British allies.

C. W. WILLIAMSON, *HISTORY OF WESTERN OHIO AND AUGLAIZE COUNTY* (COLUMBUS: W. M. LINN AND SONS, 1905)

Spemica Lawba or James Logan.

Wells and Logan were both captured as boys and adopted by their captors. Both grew to love and respect their adoptive families and tried to bridge the gap between Indian and white society. They lived their lives as men in the middle and died courageously, casualties of the conflict between the two cultures.

7

The Treaty of Greenville (1795)

When the Indians retreated at Fallen Timbers in 1794, neither General Anthony Wayne nor the Indians knew the war was over. There was nothing to suggest the skirmish by the rapids had been the final battle. Even four months later Wayne expected a return of hostilities in the spring.

Wayne's mission was to make the frontier safe for white settlement. When peace talks failed, he had invaded the heart of the Indian confederacy to force the tribes' submission. The Indians' retreat from Fallen Timbers had been a victory for his legion, but without a mutual commitment to peace, muskets and tomahawks continued to rule the region.

Wayne had demonstrated American military power. However, it was not the battle alone that convinced the chiefs to pass the peace pipe. They had also lost faith in their British allies. As they had retreated from Fallen Timbers, the commander of the British fort had refused to give them shelter. Then, two months later, the United States and Britain signed Jay's Treaty. By this treaty Britain agreed to vacate all forts on the Great Lakes. They surrendered Forts Niagara, Miamis, Detroit, and Michilimackinac to the United States government. Again the British had abandoned their Indian allies.

That winter the Indians suffered from hunger and disease. With their crops in ashes, many verged on starvation. Wayne sensed the time was right to make new overtures of peace. He sent word to all the chiefs that he would assure their safe passage to his headquarters.

Shawnee chief Blue Jacket was the first to arrive at Fort Greenville. The change of heart of his fiercest enemy was encouraging to Wayne. Before the battle at Fallen Timbers Blue Jacket had berated Miami chief Little Turtle for urging peace negotiations. Now the wily chief led the line at Wayne's door, hoping to win special favors. Wayne quickly set the time and place to conclude a treaty. He asked the Indians to meet at Greenville in mid-June.

The fort was the largest log structure in America. Wayne hoped its huge size would illustrate the might of the United States. He prepared as carefully for the peace talks as he had for his military campaign, stocking a generous supply of food and gifts for the visiting chiefs.

As the Indians arrived, he greeted them in full military finery. Early arrivals witnessed a spectacular Fourth of July celebration. On the evening of July 3 Wayne announced, "Tomorrow all the people within these lines will rejoice. . . . Do not be alarmed at the report of our big guns, they will do you no harm, they will be the harbingers of peace and gladness, and their roar will ascend into the heavens. The flag of the United States . . . shall be given to the wind to be fanned by its gentlest breeze in honor of the birthday of American freedom." Undoubtedly the Indians were impressed with the festivities.

With many groups slow to arrive, Wayne delayed the formal proceedings until July 15. By then nearly twelve hundred Indians were camped around the fort. They represented the Wyandot, Delaware, Shawnee, Ottawa, Chippewa, Potawatomi, Miami, Eel River, Wea, Kickapoo, Piankashaw, and Kaskaskia tribes.

INDIANA HISTORICAL SOCIETY, C 8117

The Signing of the Treaty of Greene Ville *by Howard Chandler Christy portrays Little Turtle addressing General Anthony Wayne and presenting him with a ceremonial wampum belt. William Wells (standing to right of Little Turtle) and William Henry Harrison (officer without hat on Wayne's right) are also depicted.*

Wayne approached the peace talks with tact and diplomacy. While recognizing Indian rights to the land they occupied, he left no doubt that he would set the terms of the treaty. Little Turtle was the only one seriously to object to Wayne's proposals. Most of the Indians, including Blue Jacket, were too anxious to curry Wayne's favor to actively challenge him.

The central part of the treaty involved setting the boundary between American and Indian territory. Wayne began by citing the boundary set in the 1789 Treaty of Fort Harmar. According to this treaty the Indians had ceded all of eastern and most of present-day southern Ohio. Wayne proposed stretching that boundary to include all of southern Ohio and a strip of present-day Indiana in the American territory.

Little Turtle protested strenuously, both to the original Fort Harmar Treaty and to the additional cession of land. He claimed the old treaty was invalid for "these lands were disposed of without our knowledge or consent." He chided the other chiefs for their easy surrender of Indian ground: "Their conduct would lead me to suppose that the Great Spirit and their forefathers had not given them the same charge that was given me, but on the contrary had directed them to sell their land to any who wore a hat as soon as he should ask it of them."

In the end the treaty established Wayne's new boundary. It also set aside sixteen tracts within the Indian territory for American forts and trading posts. In return for their land the Indians received $20,000 in trade goods with an additional $500 to $1,000 to be delivered to each tribe annually.

The treaty was concluded on August 3, 1795. Among the chiefs signing the document were Delaware chiefs Buckongahelas and Anderson, Shawnee chiefs Blue Jacket and Black Hoof, and Miami chiefs Little Turtle and Jean Baptiste Richardville. Among the Americans signing were Wayne's aide-de-camp William Henry Harrison and interpreter William Wells. All these men would continue their leading roles in the great drama playing out in the Old Northwest Territory.

The Treaty of Greenville achieved Wayne's primary goal of establishing peace on the frontier. It declared, "Henceforth all hostilities shall cease; peace is hereby established, and shall be perpetual; and a friendly intercourse shall take place between the said U.S. and Indian tribes." The Indians accepted the treaty in good faith. The chiefs who signed the treaty maintained peace with the U.S. government for the rest of their lives. Though the army blazed the way, the Treaty of Greenville was the true fulfillment of Wayne's mission.

More Treaties

The Treaty of Greenville described the large area left to the Indians:

> The United States relinquish their claims to all other Indian lands north ward of the river Ohio, eastward of the Mississippi, and westward and southward of the Great Lakes.

And it promised they might stay on it for as long as they desired:

> The Indian tribes who have a right to those lands, are quietly to enjoy them, hunting, planting, and dwelling thereon, so long as they please, without any molestation from the United States; but when those tribes, or any of them, shall be disposed to sell their lands, or any part of them, they are to be sold only to the United States.

What the Indians did not realize was that a disposition to sell could be created whenever the United States had a desire to buy. When settlers pushing west demanded more land, the government did whatever it took to convince the tribes to sell. The Indians were continually forced to make way for American expansion.

Harrison became governor of the new Indiana Territory in 1800. Three years later, President Thomas Jefferson gave him authority to make treaties with the Indians and told Harrison to buy their land as quickly as possible. Harrison vigorously pursued his duty and concluded his first treaty in June

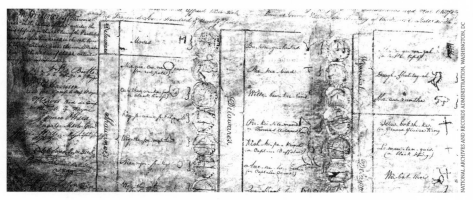

This is the third and final page of the first Treaty of Greenville. Indians placed their seals as their signatures next to their translated names. On this page there are signatures from the Shawnee, Wyandot, and Delaware.

NATIONAL ARCHIVES AND RECORDS ADMINISTRATION, WASHINGTON, DC

1803. By the Treaty of Fort Wayne the Indians ceded the area surrounding the new capital of Vincennes. For their land they received an annuity of 159 bushels of salt.

In August 1804, by the Treaty of Vincennes, Harrison bought land in southern Indiana along the Ohio River. Many squatters already lived there. He hoped buying the land would prevent trouble between the squatters and the Indians. Less than two months later he concluded the Treaty of Saint Louis. For a $1,000 annuity the Sauk and Fox tribes ceded most of Illinois north of the Illinois River, part of southern Wisconsin, and a section of northeast Missouri.

On July 4, 1805, the Ohio tribes sold a tract in northern Ohio adjoining the Greenville Treaty Line. Blue Jacket and Black Hoof both signed the treaty. A month later Harrison gained another large cession of Indiana land by the Treaty of Grouseland.

Many chiefs approved the treaties. They were commonly referred to as "government chiefs" because they carried out the wishes of the American government. Most of these chiefs probably believed that maintaining friendship with the government was essential for their tribes' survival. But signing the treaties also brought special rewards for themselves and their families.

As more treaties were completed, many tribesmen became alarmed over the steady loss of their land. At Greenville the Americans had promised the Indians that they could hold their ground forever. Yet within fifteen years their holdings had declined by millions of acres. It seemed the white men had lied, and the government chiefs appeared weak and corrupt, reaping personal profit at the expense of their tribes. Riding a rising wave of anger and resentment, new leaders such as Tecumseh and his brother, the Shawnee Prophet, gained more and more followers.

Despite Indian discontent, in 1809 Harrison decided to make another treaty. He wanted to purchase Indian lands in southern Indiana and Illinois. The Wea and Kickapoo were occupying the area. But Harrison did not approach them initially because he knew they would not wish to sell.

Instead he called Miami, Delaware, and Potawatomi chiefs to meet at Fort Wayne. The Miami were the acknowledged owners of a large part of the tract, and the Delaware used it for hunting. But the Potawatomi had no real claim. They were included because Harrison knew they were eager to increase their annuity payments.

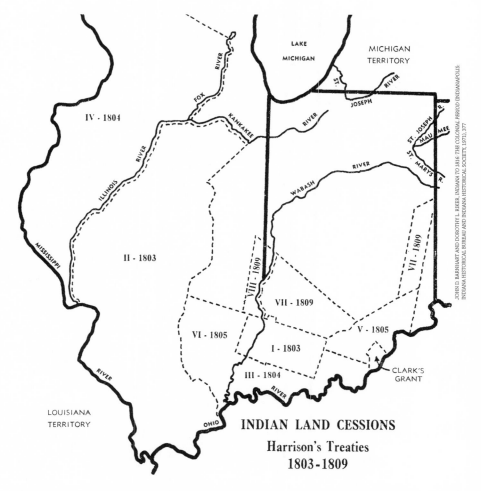

Map labels: LAKE MICHIGAN · MICHIGAN TERRITORY · ST. JOSEPH RIVER · FOX RIVER · KANKAKEE · ILLINOIS RIVER · KANKAKEE RIVER · JOSEPH · ST. JOSEPH R. · ST. MARYS R. · MAUMEE · WABASH RIVER · RIVER · MISSISSIPPI · IV - 1804 · II - 1803 · VIII - 1809 · VII - 1809 · VII - 1809 · VI - 1805 · I - 1803 · V - 1805 · III - 1804 · CLARK'S GRANT · LOUISIANA TERRITORY · OHIO · RIVER

JOHN D. BARNHART AND DOROTHY L. RIKER, *INDIANA TO 1816: THE COLONIAL PERIOD* (INDIANAPOLIS: INDIANA HISTORICAL BUREAU AND INDIANA HISTORICAL SOCIETY, 1971), 377.

INDIAN LAND CESSIONS
Harrison's Treaties
1803-1809

I.   June 7, 1803, at Fort Wayne, with the Delawares, Shawnee, Potawatomi, Miami, Eel Rivers, Wea, Kickapoo, Piankashaw, and Kaskaskia.

II.   August 13, 1803, at Vincennes, with the Kaskaskia.

III.   August 18 and 27, 1804, at Vincennes, with the Delawares and Piankashaw.

IV.   November 3, 1804, at St. Louis, with the Sauk and Foxes.

V.   August 21, 1805, at Grouseland, with the Delawares, Potawatomi, Miami, Eel Rivers, and Wea.

VI.   December 30, 1805, at Vincennes, with the Piankashaw.

VII.   September 30, 1809, at Fort Wayne, with the Delawares, Potawatomi, Miami, Eel Rivers, and Wea.

VIII.   December 9, 1809, at Vincennes, with the Kickapoo.

Between 1803 and 1809 Harrison negotiated a number of treaties with the tribes that opened vast amounts of land to white settlement.

Since the Wea were not present, Little Turtle at first objected to the sale. But pressure from the Potawatomi ultimately resulted in the Miami's approval. Then, to create pressure on the reluctant Kickapoo, the Miami and Wea were promised an additional annuity once the Kickapoo signed the treaty.

After obtaining the agreement of the Potawatomi, Delaware, and Miami chiefs, Harrison dealt with the Wea and Kickapoo the next spring. With a divide and conquer strategy, he used tribes willing to sell to pressure those wanting to hold the land. The second Treaty of Fort Wayne resulted in a new surge of settlers and an explosion of Indian hostility. With land loss and encroaching white culture, their way of life was severely threatened.

8

The Prophet (1775–1836)

My name is Tenskwatawa. You know me as the Prophet. I was chosen by the Master of Life to teach the Indians to live as He intended. My medicine was strong. Did I not darken the sun and bring back its light? But my powers did not arise in my youth. My early days were full of hardship.

Before my birth the white men killed my father. He fell defending our ground. Like him, my brothers became Shawnee warriors, but I had no one to teach me the skills of a warrior. When I tried to learn from the other boys, I lost the sight of an eye. That injury plagued me the rest of my days.

I was born one of three sons (triplets). The birth of three boys is usually a sign of the Master of Life's special favor. Yet good fortune failed to attend me. After the Long Knives burned our town, my mother went west and left me behind. I grew to manhood with neither a father's guidance nor a mother's care and affection.

After my mother left, my sister Tecumapease took my brothers and me into her dwelling. She favored Tecumseh, who was born seven years before me. Tecumseh was blessed with a strong, agile body and the admiration of all the men and boys of our village. Though I tried to be equally worthy of praise, I was shunned and called Lalawethika, "the Noisemaker." It was a name of no respect.

My oldest brother, Chiksika, also favored Tecumseh and taught him how to hunt. Because of my blindness I was left behind. As I grew older I was not invited to join their war parties. After Chiksika's death Tecumseh became a war chief. When he led his scouts to track General Arthur St. Clair's army, again I remained home and was deprived the honor of the victory.

I finally got to fight alongside my brothers three years later when we faced General Anthony Wayne at the Battle of Fallen Timbers. Tecumseh and I escaped with our lives, but our brother, Sauwauseekau, was struck down by the white men. I had now lost my father and two brothers to the spawn of the Evil Spirit.

After the battle I followed Tecumseh from camp to camp for many years. Finally we settled along the White River among the Delaware. I often returned from the hunt empty-handed, leaving my family hungry. I cursed the white men who had wasted our game and the misfortune that cost me an eye. I was a man without respect or honor.

Seeking a more useful life, I became a medicine man. I learned from an old man known for gifts of prophecy and healing. After his death a terrible illness swept through our village. I used all the herbs and words he had taught me but could not halt the dying. I was cast down by my failure. One night, after many hours of drinking, I fell into a deep sleep before the fire. When my wife and neighbors found me, they took me for dead. They began preparing my body for burial. But before they finished, I awoke.

I had returned from a long journey to the Spirit World. There I had seen a land abundant in fish and game and fields of golden corn. It was a special land reserved for those who had lived their lives as the Master of Life intended. I also saw a dark and frightening place. It was a land of pain and torture, where the unworthy suffered and burned until they had atoned for their sins.

After sharing my vision I vowed to abandon my old ways. Never again did my lips touch the white man's whiskey. I began my life anew and became known as Tenskwatawa, the "Open Door." I would lead my people to the land of plenty in the Spirit World.

As seasons passed I was gifted with many visions and prophecies. The Master of Life called me to make my village at Greenville. There I would share his words. I reclaimed a piece of ground seized from the Indians there.

News of my revelations spread through all the Indian villages. In the summer hundreds of warriors, their women, and their children came to hear me. They traveled great distances. Some came from the shores of great lakes in the north, others from the prairies of the west. My message united warriors of many tribes. Delaware, Wyandot, Potawatomi, Kickapoo, Ottawa, Chippewa, Winnebago, Saus, and Miami mingled with my Shawnee kinsmen.

Every night I spoke in the council house. I taught how to live as the Master of Life intended. I explained that the Long Knives had not been made like red men, but were spawn of the Evil Spirit. To please the Master of Life, the Indians must turn away from white men. They must return to the ways of our ancestors.

Like me, they must give up whiskey. The white man's drink is poison to us. They must eat wild game and fish, rather than hogs and cattle. They must wear skins, not cloth, and use stone and wood tools, not those of iron. If the Indians would please the Master of Life, he would restore to us our ancient

INDIANA HISTORICAL SOCIETY

Portrait of Tenskwatawa, the Shawnee Prophet.

ground, with the bones of the Long Knives beneath it.

White men feared my influence. Governor William Henry Harrison tried to turn my people against me. He called me a "pretended prophet" and challenged me to prove my powers. The proof was not long in coming. I announced a day for the people to gather—June 16, 1806. On that day I promised to blacken the midday sun. When the day arrived, I remained in my lodge all morning, calling on the Master of Life to fulfill my prophecy. As the sky darkened, the onlookers trembled. I came from my lodge to calm them and vowed to recall the sun to its former splendor. As light returned, the people were filled with awe. News of my strong medicine soon reached all the Indian towns.

White men were filled with terror. Had one of their race ever turned the sun black and then restored its glory? They cried out to their chiefs to subdue me. William Wells called me to Fort Wayne to hear a message from his president. I was enraged! Why did Wells not come to me? I would not answer the summons of such a trifling white man.

The governor of Ohio, Thomas Kirker, showed me greater respect. He sent his highest officials to me at Greenville. In return I sent a delegation of my most important chiefs to Chillicothe. Leading the party were Blue Jacket and Tecumseh.

While they were gone, I remained at Greenville to receive my visitors. One visitor was Main Poc of the Potawatomi, who was known in the West as a chief of strong medicine. No arrow or bullet could harm him. Main Poc heard my words and became a fierce ally. He invited me to build a village on his land by the Tippecanoe River. There I would be closer to my western followers and away from troublesome white men.

After consulting the Master of Life, I led my people to our new home. Away from white influence I would return them to our ancestors' ways. Little Turtle and other bad chiefs tried to stop me. Like white men, they feared my power. But their threats could not harm me for my medicine was strong. From my village in the West I would unite all the Indians.

Once my town was established I went to meet Harrison. He was impressed by my words. I assured him the Master of Life made the Indians for good, not evil, and commanded we live in peace. My warriors would not raise their hatchets against him. I convinced him that Wells and Little Turtle spread lies for their own selfish purposes.

Yet evil white men and government chiefs still plotted against me. The governor heard their words. He schemed with them to take more of our ground. He accused my followers of many false crimes. Finally, he led an army against me. I could not ignore his aggression. His army camped in sight of my village, causing great alarm among our women and children.

Tecumseh was not home to defend us. He was in the South, gathering Indians of many tribes to join us. Though I am unseasoned in the ways of war like my brother, I have strong medicine. I had to lead my warriors in battle. The Master of Life would surely guarantee our victory over the invading army.

We attacked Harrison's camp before dawn. I watched my warriors fight while calling on the Master of Life for their protection. But my medicine failed. Many warriors died. I could not understand why the Master of Life had abandoned me.

*I grieve for my faithless people. What will become of them? The Master of
Life chose me to lead them to reclaim the land of our ancestors. Without my
strong medicine, I fear they will not succeed.*

~ Tenskwatawa, 1811

Following the battle with Harrison's troops at Tippecanoe, the Prophet
lost most of his influence. Upon returning home Tecumseh took the lead
in the struggle against white expansion. Later, during the War of 1812, the
Prophet avoided most of the fighting and fled to Canada. He ended his exile
in 1824 and participated in the Shawnee removal to Kansas. In 1836 he died
there, largely ignored and forgotten by both his own people and the American
government.

Beware of Witches

The Prophet warned his followers to beware of those who practiced witchcraft. He taught that witches, like Long Knives, were agents of the Evil Spirit
and must be destroyed. Anyone closely associated with the Long Knives or
opposed to Tenskwatawa was suspected of witchcraft.

Indians who had converted to Christianity were frequently accused. One
such victim was Joshua Jr., a Moravian Christian Indian. Thirty years earlier
Joshua had played the spinet for church services at Gnadenhutten. In 1782
his two oldest daughters died in the massacre there. Despite the tragedy
Joshua had maintained his faith and served the missionaries as a musician,
interpreter, and carpenter.

In 1806 Joshua was living in a Delaware village in eastern Indiana. Many
there had become disciples of the Prophet. Desiring to please the Master of
Life, they seized a dozen Indians believed to be witches, one of whom was
Joshua. The Prophet arrived at the Delaware village on March 15 to judge the
accused. With great ceremony he stared into the face of each prisoner and pro-
nounced guilt or innocence. He declared Joshua guilty. Like the unfortunate
victims of Gnadenhutten, the innocent man soon met his executioners. He
was tomahawked twice before being burned at the stake.

A later victim of the Prophet's witch hunts was an elderly Wyandot tribesman. He was called Leatherlips by neighboring white men in recognition of his

honesty. His friendship with the Long Knives and opposition to the Prophet marked him as a witch. In June 1810 the Prophet sent six warriors from his Tippecanoe village to execute the old man. They found him in his hunting camp on the Scioto River, just north of present-day Columbus, Ohio.

Word of Leatherlips's "trial" reached the white community, and several men came to watch. Leatherlips was charged with causing sickness among members of his tribe. After two or three hours of deliberation the sentence of death was announced. One of the white men tried to save Leatherlips's life by offering a horse in trade for his release. The offer was rejected, and the condemned man prepared for death.

Leatherlips ate a meal of jerked venison, put on his best clothes, and painted his face. After shaking hands with white spectators he marched toward his grave, chanting his death song on the way. He knelt and solemnly prayed to the Great Spirit. The leader of the executioners, Wyandot chief Roundhead, also knelt and prayed.

Suddenly one of the warriors sprang forward, raised his tomahawk, and struck a blow to Leatherlips's head. The old man did not die immediately but lay in silent agony. Sweat gathered on his neck and brow. Finally, after three more blows, his lifeless body was shoved into the grave and quickly buried.

The Prophet's new religion eclipsed traditional rivalries and united Indians from many tribes and villages. By executing witches, the Prophet used religious doctrine to eliminate political enemies. His spiritual authority brought him great political power as well.

Sculpture honoring Leatherlips in Dublin, Ohio, near the place of his execution and burial.

9

The Battle of Tippecanoe (1811)

In December 1810 Governor William Henry Harrison wrote to Secretary of War William Eustis of the need to secure more Indian land. "The little tract which was purchased to the west of the Greenville boundary will be soon filled up to the very line and our backwoods men are not of a disposition to content themselves with land of an inferior quality when they see in their immediate neighbourhood the finest country as to soil in the world occupied by a few wretched savages," Harrison noted. While Harrison wanted to open more Indian land for white settlement, the Shawnee brothers, Tecumseh and the Prophet, were building an Indian confederacy to challenge American expansion. In 1808 they had established Prophetstown at the junction of the Wabash and Tippecanoe Rivers. Indians from many tribes gathered there, which made Prophetstown the center of Indian resistance.

In July 1811 Tecumseh went to Vincennes. It was his second visit to the governor. He had already united the northern Indian tribes and was traveling south to add southern warriors to his force. Harrison feared Tecumseh's growing power since it would be harder to purchase Indian land with the tribes united in opposition, and a strong Indian confederacy posed a serious military threat. Sporadic Indian raids had already discouraged new settlement.

Harrison decided to strike while Tecumseh was away in the South. Eustis granted him permission to march on Prophetstown but wanted the Indians dispersed without bloodshed. Eustis hoped the mere sight of American troops would cause them to flee.

Harrison began his campaign on September 26, 1811. He led a force of a thousand men, including army regulars, Indiana militiamen, and Kentucky volunteers. Though he had served as General Anthony Wayne's aide, Harrison had never commanded in battle. He recruited experienced staff to help him.

They were trusted friends, political allies, and business associates. All shared his passion for opening land to American settlement.

Following Wayne's example, Harrison advanced slowly, carefully securing his supply network. He built a large fort and infirmary north of present-day Terre Haute and a blockhouse at the junction of the Wabash and Big Vermilion Rivers. In late October he made a final attempt to negotiate peace. He promised to withdraw if his demands were met. Among his demands were the expulsion of Potawatomi, Kickapoo, and Winnebago warriors from Prophetstown, the return of stolen horses, and the surrender of warriors guilty of crimes against the white men.

When the Prophet did not comply, Harrison began his final advance. The army reached the outskirts of the village on the afternoon of November 6, and Harrison ordered his troops into battle position, prepared to attack. The steady approach of the American army had thrown the Indians into a state of turmoil. Some warriors had already left the village. With Tecumseh absent, the Prophet alone was in charge. He carefully weighed his options. He could submit to Harrison and abandon the village, or he could lead his warriors against the American army.

Fighting Harrison's army risked defeat and the collapse of the entire Indian confederacy. Tecumseh had warned the Prophet to avoid conflict until his return since he was not a skilled warrior and the confederacy was not ready to challenge American military power.

Yet submitting to Harrison would discredit the Prophet in the eyes of his followers. It would be a sign of weakness. He and his brother had taught the tribes to stand up to the white men, and their young warriors were eager to strike. If the Prophet urged caution, they might turn to bolder leaders.

When the army came within sight, the Prophet decided he must respond to the aggression. However, he did not want to fight in the open fields. Since his warriors were outnumbered, he needed to surprise the Americans.

He sent out a warrior with a white flag to meet Harrison's scouts. The warrior announced that the Prophet desired peace and would meet Harrison the next morning to return some stolen horses. Harrison reluctantly agreed to a cease-fire. He did not believe the Indians had peaceful intentions but could not ignore Eustis's order to avoid bloodshed.

The army made camp on a high narrow ridge a mile west of the village. To the west was an embankment covered with brush and to the east, an area of tall grass. Both sides offered cover for enemy approach, but Harrison did not expect the Indians to attack in darkness. He did not order construction of barricades or trenches that night.

Above all he wanted his men well rested. If the Prophet refused his demands the next morning he planned to attack the village. Harrison retired to his tent, with orders for his men to sleep on their weapons and arise before daylight. As the night progressed, a cold rain fell on the camp, and fires were kindled to warm the resting troops.

While Harrison slept, the Prophet communed with the spirits. He assured his followers that he had strong medicine. The white men's bullets could not harm them since rain would dampen their powder. And though it would be too dark for the white men to see, the Indians would have light to aim their weapons.

He told the warriors that the Master of Life required Harrison's death. While Harrison lived, the Long Knives could not be defeated. But without him, his soldiers would scatter like frightened birds. The Prophet appointed a group of marksmen to enter the camp and kill Harrison. The rest of the warriors would follow and claim the victory.

By cover of darkness the Indians crept through the grass and brush to surround the sleeping soldiers. Rain fell and flames from campfires illumined the camp. The warriors gained confidence. Two of the Prophet's promises had been fulfilled. The white men's powder was ruined and the Indians could easily see their targets.

At 4:15 a.m. the assassins assigned to kill Harrison slipped into the camp. An alert sentry fired a shot of alarm. A few warriors reached the officers' tents, but by then Harrison had mounted a horse. However, he had not mounted his usual light grey mare, which had broken loose. Instead, Harrison mounted his aide's dark stallion and rode out to rally his troops, accompanied by an officer on a white horse. Spotting the light colored horse, a warrior shot the officer, mistaking him for Harrison.

As the fighting raged, the Prophet watched from a safe distance west of the battle. He chanted and drummed to summon magic and encourage his warriors. Arrows and bullets rained down on the white men, caught in the spotlight of fire. But soon the flames were extinguished, and both sides fought blindly. As day broke, Sam Wells, brother of William, led his mounted volunteers on a counterattack.

After nearly two hours the Indians' powder ran low. When the sun lifted their cover of darkness, they withdrew to Prophetstown. Nearly fifty warriors

An 1889 lithograph of a painting by Alonzo Chappel depicting the Battle of Tippecanoe.

lay dead with many more wounded. They cursed the Prophet for deceiving them. His magic had not stopped the white men's bullets. They no longer believed in his special powers. They spared his life but hurriedly left Prophetstown.

As Harrison surveyed the wreckage of the battlefield, it was clear that though the Indians had retreated, it was hardly a victory. Forty-six of his men were dead and 151 were seriously injured. Many of the casualties were his close friends and prominent frontier citizens. Harrison belatedly ordered construction of a barricade and trench around the camp. The next morning he sent scouts to survey the Indian village. They found it deserted except for one old woman. They did not harm the woman but burned the town to the ground after seizing its stores of corn and beans.

Because of the large number of casualties, Harrison was heavily criticized. Some said he should have attacked immediately, rather than agreeing to meet the Prophet the next morning. Others faulted him for not reinforcing the camp before retiring for the night. A few believed the whole expedition was misguided. In the following weeks Harrison focused his attention on countering his critics. He desperately worked to save his reputation. His friends persuaded the Kentucky legislature to pass a resolution commending him. In the end most frontier citizens praised him for fighting the Indians.

Despite questionable military decisions, Harrison did achieve the short-term goal of his campaign. The Prophet was discredited and his town abandoned. Returning home in January, Tecumseh found Prophetstown in ruins and his confederation splintered. In the long term, however, Harrison's strike added more fuel to the fire of Indian resentment. Violence increased on the frontier, and many young warriors joined Tecumseh to fight the Americans.

William Henry Harrison

In 1840 Harrison was elected president of the United States. He was the first presidential candidate to have a campaign slogan: "Tippecanoe and Tyler, too." The slogan enhanced his image as a rugged Indian fighter of the old frontier. He became known as "Old Tip," the hero of the Battle of Tippecanoe. A rally at the battle site drew 60,000 people.

When Harrison died a month after taking office, his vice president, John Tyler, became president. Harrison's term was the shortest in American history. But his brief term followed the longest inaugural address. Harrison gave his two-hour speech on a cold, damp day in March. True to his rugged reputation, the sixty-eight-year-old president wore no coat or hat. Afterward he developed pneumonia and died.

Though Harrison campaigned as a simple frontiersman, the image was misleading. He had always been a man of ample means. While governor of the Indiana Territory, he lived in the frontier town of Vincennes. But he did not live in a crude log cabin. He and his family lived in a large brick mansion called Grouseland.

Harrison was the son of a wealthy plantation owner who was elected three times as the governor of Virginia. William was well educated and studied medicine. But the life of a physician did not suit his restless nature. At the age of eighteen he left medicine for a military career. He hoped to make a name for himself on the American frontier.

Through a family friend, George Washington, Harrison secured a position as an officer in the infantry. He was assigned to Fort Washington in the Northwest Territory. Harrison's enthusiasm and hard work soon drew the notice of General Anthony Wayne. He became Wayne's aide and served by his side through the Battle of Fallen Timbers and the treaty negotiations at Greenville. After Wayne's death in 1796 Harrison became Fort Washington's commander.

Two years later Harrison resigned to pursue greater ambitions. Harrison became secretary of the Northwest Territory. He was then elected as the territory's first delegate to Congress. He promised to open the western frontier to ambitious men such as himself who longed for land and opportunity. The Harrison Land Act of 1800 made it easier for citizens to buy homesteads in the Old Northwest. Harrison's legislation allowed them to buy smaller tracts of land and pay for them in installments.

Harrison was appointed governor of the newly formed Indiana Territory in 1800. He served as governor for twelve years until taking command of the Northwestern American forces during the War of 1812. In 1803 President Thomas Jefferson gave Harrison the authority to make treaties with the Indians. He instructed him to acquire titles to as much Indian land as possible. With Jefferson's encouragement, Harrison relentlessly pursued that goal, sometimes through questionable means (see Chapter 7).

Harrison was sympathetic to the plight of the Indians. He saw the harmful effects of alcohol on the Indians and tried to limit its sale. However, his greater loyalty was to the expansion of the United States, so he looked the other way when spirits were used to gain Indian approval of treaties ceding their land.

When present-day Indiana was separated from the rest of the territory in 1809, Harrison redoubled his efforts for settlement. He hoped to quickly reach the population required for statehood— at least 20,000 free inhabitants (slavery was banned in the territory but indentured servitude was legal at this time). The growing power of Tecumseh and the Prophet frustrated his efforts by frightening settlers away. Harrison's campaign to destroy Prophetstown was the culmination of his efforts to rid the area of the Shawnee brothers' influence.

Harrison performed his duties as he saw them with diligence and conviction. He was an ambitious man who merged his drive for personal power with his vision of the public good. As both a military and political leader, he was a driving force in American expansion and the concurrent decline of the Indians of the Old Northwest.

William Henry Harrison.

10

Tecumseh (1768–1813)

I am told that on the night of my birth a bright star flashed across the sky. My father knew it was "the panther that crosses the sky," the spirit animal of our clan. So I was given the spirit's name, Tecumseh.

When I was six my father led our warriors into battle. The red tomahawk passed from village to village as an army of white men marched toward us. The holy men chanted and beat their drums. The warriors painted their bodies and fasted. As they left our town they whooped and fired their weapons.

My brother Chiksika went with my father. He was fourteen. I was proud of my father and brother and wished I could go, too. My father did not return. He fell as a Shawnee warrior. Chiksika vowed to avenge his death. As our father lay dying, Chiksika promised to teach me the ways of a warrior and lead me against the white men.

The following years were full of smoke. Many times the Long Knives burned our villages. When my mother grew weary of smoke and death, she left us and moved west. But my brothers and I stayed behind. I was eleven and my brothers Lalawethika (the Prophet) and Kumskaukau but five. The younger boys feared the Long Knives, but I yearned to fight them. I fed my craving for battle by playing games of war with my friends. Sometimes Kumskaukau would join us, but Lalawethika merely shouted from behind the bushes.

I often followed Chiksika on the hunt. We would leave the village for many days, crossing the Ohio River to our hunting grounds beyond. Chiksika taught me to be a man. There was never a braver warrior than my brother. He was held in respect by all the men of our village.

When I was fourteen I finally followed him into battle. Again the Long Knives had marched up the valley to destroy our towns. While the women and children ran to the hills, I stayed to fight. My courage fled, however, at the sight of my wounded brother's blood. I was shamed by my cowardice. I vowed I never again would run from the enemy.

When General Benjamin Logan invaded our village four years later, I did not flee, despite the sight of blood. When one of his men sunk a hatchet deep in the skull of Chief Moluntha, it only increased my will to fight. The old man had signed a treaty with the Long Knives just months before his murder. The American flag flew beside his dwelling. Moluntha's blood colored my rage bright red for years to come.

The next year I followed Chiksika south. We went to help fight the Long Knives who intruded on Cherokee ground. I was gone more than three years. By the time I returned, I had gained much knowledge of war but lost my brother. He had also been my closest friend. Like our father, he died the honorable death of a warrior. I vowed to become as noble and as brave as Chiksika.

As I traveled home I heard of the Indian victory at Kekionga. Blue Jacket had led our Shawnee warriors in defense of Indian ground. I went to join him.

The next year we defeated another army of Long Knives. Little Turtle with his Miami and Buckongahelas with the Delaware shared in the victory. A single tribe, like a lone stick, is easily broken; united tribes, like a bundle of sticks, are strong. With the tribes united, we had forced the Long Knives from our soil.

Shamed by defeat, the Americans sent a larger army against us. It was led by General Anthony Wayne. Warriors from many tribes came to defend our land. But when the army finally attacked us, most were away seeking food. There were at least six Long Knives for every Indian.

I fought beside my brothers. The Long Knives charged us with their blades. But despite our small numbers, we fought back. With our ammunition spent, we sought shelter within Fort Miamis, but the British turned us away. We were forced to retreat to the shores of the lake to prepare for the next battle.

Wayne camped in the shadow of the British fort. While the fort's commander had refused us shelter, he allowed the Long Knives to rest undisturbed. He allowed them to taunt his men and raid his stores of grain. The Redcoats were cowardly allies. They could not be trusted.

The next battle never came. Instead, the Long Knives left the Glaize and set fire to our fields and towns from there to Kekionga. We suffered our defeat. With corn turned black, food was scarce for the Indians.

I led my warriors south to hunt in the land of our childhood. Soon I had nearly two hundred followers. The next summer, when Wayne called us to Greenville, we did not go. There could be no lasting peace with men who had ravaged our land and murdered our women and children.

Tecumseh, wearing a European-style jacket and what appears to be a Jefferson medal.

For the next few years we moved from place to place. At the invitation of the Delaware I established a village on the White River beyond the treaty line. The surrounding forests and streams met our needs. Despite our distance from white men, their evils continued to plague us.

When drinking the traders' whiskey, many warriors fought each other and struck their wives. They passed many days in a drunken stupor. My own brother, Lalawethika, was among the worst afflicted. When he failed as a hunter, I had to bring meat to his family. I encouraged him to learn the skills of a healer, hoping this work would better suit him.

At that time our people were dying in large numbers. Though my brother chanted and made many potions, he could not save them. His medicine was too weak. But one night he fell into a deep stupor and had a vision. The Master of Life called him to teach the Indians to reclaim our ancestors' ways.

My brother became Tenskwatawa, the "Open Door." He no longer drank firewater nor neglected his family. His medicine was strong. Indians from many tribes traveled to see him.

When the Master of Life told him to gather the Indians near Greenville, I built a village there. Our new town caused much unease among the Long Knives. They feared my brother's power and the growing number of warriors around him.

Some Indians also feared my brother. They tried to discredit him. Many of his enemies were chiefs who had joined hands with the American government. They sold our land for favors and took on ways of the white men. Miami chief Little Turtle and William Wells sold Indian ground to fill their own bags with silver. Our Shawnee brother, Black Hoof, destroyed our warriors' manhood, trading war clubs and muskets for shovels and plows. It is no wonder the Master of Life was angry.

During three years at Greenville I told the Long Knives many times we meant them no harm. My band committed no crimes against them. But Wells and Black Hoof spread lies about us.

I finally moved my band far from the new white settlements. We traveled deep into Indian territory, moving west along the Wabash River. In the spring of 1808 I established a new village on ground near the mouth of the Tippecanoe River. We built nearly two hundred dwellings and a House of the Strangers for those who came to hear Tenskwatawa. Our village became known as Prophetstown.

Though we tried to remove ourselves from white men, their thirst for our land increased. Governor William Henry Harrison plotted to swallow more of our ground. He asked the Indians to meet at Fort Wayne. He planned to make another treaty. Again white settlers would be at our door.

I knew the time had come for the Indians to stand their ground. If we did not halt the Americans soon, we would have no ground to stand on. We would be pushed farther and farther until we drowned in the lakes to the north or river to the west. Again, I worked to bind all the tribes together, like sticks in a bundle. I traveled north and south and east and west to unite the tribes in defense of our common ground.

Late in the summer of 1809 I met with the warriors at Wapakoneta. This was the home of Black Hoof. I was distressed by the sight of men tending corn. It was an insult to the Master of Life.

I met the young men in the council house and spoke my mind. I implored them to throw down their plows and join me at Prophetstown. In the midst of our gathering, a paper came from Harrison regarding his talks at Fort Wayne. I cast it into the fire and vowed that if he were there himself, I would dispatch him in the same way.

The warriors shouted their approval. By the next spring they poured into Prophetstown. They were angry about the treaty that had been made at Fort Wayne. Once again Harrison had bribed a few bad chiefs to sell our land. The land was not theirs to sell. Twice I went to Harrison and spoke for many tribes. I said he must return our land. I told him we might be friends if he returned it, but he did not choose the path of peace. Instead, he gathered an army and marched on our town. I was away, and my brother foolishly tried to fight. Tenskwatawa had agreed to avoid all conflict until I returned with warriors from all the tribes. I had hoped that seeing the tribes united, the Americans might surrender our ground without a clash of guns and tomahawks.

When I found our town in ashes, I was filled with bitterness for the man who had wrought such destruction. But Harrison was never a man to be trusted. My greater wrath was aimed at my brother who allowed his pride to destroy our plans. Even the Master of Life was angry, shaking the ground, again and again.

I must move quickly to rebuild our alliance. The American army may come again. Some of my warriors have returned, but many more are needed. I will once more call on all the tribes to join us. I have already sent messengers on to Fort Malden to ask for British powder.

War or peace is in Harrison's hands. He must return the lands stolen in his fraudulent treaties. The Americans must retreat to the boundary agreed upon at Greenville. If our demands are not met, the rivers will run red with the Long Knives' blood, and their bones will turn white on our ground.

~ Tecumseh (1812)

Tecumseh Confronts William Henry Harrison

On August 12, 1810, eighty Indian canoes pulled ashore near Vincennes, Indiana Territory. Tecumseh had come to face his greatest adversary, William Henry Harrison the governor of the Indiana Territory, who was the chief agent of the U.S. government's policy of expansion and rapid white settlement. Tecumseh was the leader of the Indian resistance. He had come to voice complaints about the recent Treaty of Fort Wayne. With this treaty the Indians had surrendered three million more acres.

The meeting took place outside the governor's mansion. Harrison and his men sat on a platform in the clearing of a small grove of walnut trees. When Tecumseh was offered a chair, the proud warrior replied, "The earth [is] the most proper place for the Indians, as they [like] to repose upon the bosom of their mother." With that the Indians dropped to the ground, and the meeting began.

Speeches lasted several days. Tecumseh detailed a long list of American offenses, including the Gnadenhutten Massacre and the murder of Chief Moluntha. He stated that no Indian lands could be sold without consent of all the tribes, making the Treaty of Fort Wayne invalid. Only a few chiefs had signed, and they did not represent the will of their people. Harrison countered that the Indians had always been treated justly and their lands purchased fairly.

At one dramatic moment, Tecumseh jumped to his feet and shouted angrily. According to the interpreter, Tecumseh had called Harrison a liar. Harrison's soldiers sprang forward. Tecumseh's warriors seized their knives and war clubs. Drawing his own sword, Harrison calmly regarded his adversary. He then ordered his men to lower their weapons and abruptly ended the meeting.

The next day, when tempers had cooled, talks resumed. But it was obvious that there would be no agreement. Speaking of the land, Tecumseh said, "No tribe has the right to sell [the land], even to each other, much less strangers. . . . Sell a country! Why not sell the air, the great sea, as well as the earth? Did not the Great Spirit make them all for the use of his children?"

Despite their opposing positions, Harrison expressed respect for his adversary. Writing to Secretary of War William Eustis in August 1811, Harrison said, "The implicit obedience and respect which the followers of Tecumseh pay to him is really astonishing and more than any other circumstance bespeaks him one of those uncommon geniuses, which spring up oc-

The confrontation between Tecumseh and William Henry Harrison in August 1810 in the walnut grove at Harrison's home, Grouseland, in Vincennes, Indiana Territory.

casionally to produce revolutions and overturn the established order of things. . . . You see him today on the Wabash and in a short time you hear of him on the shores of Lake Erie or Michigan, or on the banks of the Mississippi and wherever he goes he makes an impression favorable to his purposes."

But respect was not enough to avert war. Tecumseh and Harrison presented vastly different views of Indian-white relations, as well as of their relationship with the land. Their views could not be reconciled. They eventually met on the battlefield.

When the United States declared war on Great Britain in June 1812, Tecumseh joined his Indian forces with those of the British. He died at the Battle of the Thames on October 5, 1813, near present-day Chatham, Ontario. His death marked the end of united Indian resistance to American expansion. Following the death of their leader, the tribes of the confederacy surrendered to Harrison at Detroit. At the conclusion of the war, the Indians were forced to sign treaties ceding large tracts of their remaining land.

11

The War of 1812 (1812–1815)

After William Henry Harrison's raid on Prophetstown in late 1811, Indian hostility escalated. When President James Madison stated the case for war with Great Britain on June 1, 1812, he blamed the British for instigating Indian violence on the frontier. He also cited British interference with American trade with Europe and the seizure of American sailors from merchant ships to serve in the Royal Navy.

The United States officially declared war on June 12, 1812. Tecumseh gained a powerful ally when the British went to war with the United States. With the help of British forces he hoped to reclaim lost Indian land. The situation was chaotic. Some Indians joined the American army, while others joined Tecumseh to fight against it. The settlers did not know a friendly Indian from a hostile one and were frightened.

Under the influence of Delaware chief Anderson and his son-in-law William Conner, most Delaware maintained peace with the American government, but the Shawnee were divided. Many of Tecumseh's tribesmen served his archenemy, Harrison, who was the new commander of the Army of the Northwest. Unfortunately, Indian recruits were often abused by their white comrades. While serving with the American army Shawnee chief Black Hoof was shot in the face by a white militiaman. Black Hoof recovered, but once again Indian goodwill had been met with malice. Like the Shawnee, Miami loyalties were split. After American troops destroyed their villages, warriors who had opposed Tecumseh and the Prophet fought to defend their homes.

In September 1812 news of an Indian massacre at Pigeon Roost caused great alarm across the frontier. Pigeon Roost was a small, white community in southern Indiana, and most of its families had settled there a few years earlier. Their contact with Indians had been infrequent but friendly. When the raid occurred, some of the men were away on militia duty. In their absence three men, five women, and sixteen children were murdered by Indian warriors. As news of the killing spread, settlers rushed to the nearest blockhouse for protection.

Assaults on Fort Wayne and Fort Harrison quickly followed the massacre. Older Miami chiefs tried to restrain their warriors, but some of the younger men were eager to join the fight. Both forts withstood attack. Nevertheless, Harrison retaliated by burning Miami villages on the Eel and Wabash Rivers. Though the majority of Miami chiefs had maintained their neutrality, Harrison regarded the entire tribe as the enemy.

Detroit fell to the British in August and with it the Michigan Territory. When Harrison became commander of the Army of the Northwest that September, his major objective was to recover the lost ground. This proved to be a long and difficult task. On January 22, 1813, a force of British and Indian troops defeated his army at the River Raisin, near present-day Monroe, Michigan. Nearly four hundred Americans died, and five hundred more were wounded or captured.

After the battle, British troops departed quickly for Fort Malden, across the frozen Detroit River. They took those captives who could walk, but they left the injured behind. The British commander, General Henry Procter, promised to return the next day with sleds for the remaining prisoners. Unfortunately, by the time the sleds arrived the Indians had slaughtered many of the wounded Americans. The cry, "Remember the River Raisin!", rallied American troops throughout the rest of the war.

The defeat at the River Raisin forced Harrison to postpone his Detroit campaign. He turned to rebuilding the army, training new recruits, and securing his supply lines. He was determined to follow the patient approach of his mentor, General Anthony Wayne.

Throughout the winter of 1813, Harrison's troops erected Fort Meigs. It became a massive structure with a stockade enclosing ten acres. The new fort was located on the Maumee River across from the site of the Battle of Fallen Timbers. It served as Harrison's base to retake Michigan and launch an invasion of Canada.

In April Procter and Tecumseh led a British-Indian force of 2,200 toward the new fort. They set up their camp across the river near old Fort Miamis and placed artillery along the river bank. On May 1 they began to shell the American fort. In response, Harrison ordered Kentucky militiamen under Colonel William Dudley to cross the water and disable the guns.

COURTESY OF ELIZABETH O'MALEY

Cannon fortify the walls at the re-created Fort Meigs in Perrysburgh, Ohio. The original fort was built during the War of 1812 withstood two sieges and served as Harrison's headquarters.

Some of Dudley's men exceeded their orders and chased Indian warriors into the woods. They were no match for the Indians. Only a few of the Americans escaped the forest maze—most were captured. Of Dudley's 900 men, only 150 returned to Fort Meigs.

The captives were marched to Fort Miamis. Outside the fort's gate the Indian warriors formed a tunnel of two lines and forced the prisoners to run the gauntlet, striking their victims with clubs and tomahawks as they rushed by. Greater affliction followed inside the fort. The warriors fired muskets into the crowd of captives and ripped off their scalps. British officers could not re-gain control. Several Americans died before Tecumseh arrived and stopped the carnage. Tecumseh condemned the torture of prisoners. It is said he turned to Procter and scolded: "You are unfit to command. Go and put on petticoats!"

Unable to penetrate Fort Meigs, the British and the Indians retreated on May 9. The fort had survived the attack. But over the course of the siege American casualties had been heavy: 160 dead, 190 wounded, and 630 cap-tured. The war was not going well for Harrison. Yet he continued to prepare for his campaign to Detroit and beyond. He methodically strengthened his line of forts and assembled supplies.

Harrison's big break came with Oliver Hazard Perry's naval victory at the Battle of Lake Erie. In August 1813 Perry brought seven ships past the British blockade, and on September 10 he won control of the lake. He gave Harrison the news in his famous message: "We have met the enemy and they are ours."

Harrison's troops met Perry's ships at present-day Port Clinton, Ohio, and loaded sixteen vessels and ninety barges to sail for British Fort Malden, across the river from Detroit. Meanwhile, allied Shawnee scouts led additional Ameri-can troops by land from Fort Meigs. They arrived on September 30 to join the force that had come by water.

Anticipating Harrison's arrival, Procter started retreating up the Thames River. Tecumseh was enraged at Procter's desertion. Just as at Fort Miamis nineteen years earlier, the British had abandoned the Indians. In a speech to Procter, Tecumseh exclaimed: "Father! You have got the arms and ammunition which our great father sent for his red children. If you have an idea of going away, give them to us. . . . We are determined to defend our lands, and if it is His will we wish to leave our bones upon them." Though greatly outmanned, Tecumseh was determined to fight Harrison to the death.

With his troops at Detroit and Procter's retreat, Harrison had accom-plished his immediate goal, the recovery of the Michigan Territory. But his thoughts returned to the major focus of his entire political career—securing land for white settlement. He saw his chance to crush Indian resistance to American expansion forever. He set out to meet his chief adversary, Tecumseh, on the field of battle.

Harrison's army followed the retreating enemy troops. He caught up with them near Moraviantown, a village built by the missionaries who had founded Gnadenhutten many years before. Harrison's troops numbered nearly 3,700 men. They faced 800 British regulars and 500 warriors led by Tecumseh. The American army easily won a decisive victory at the Battle of the Thames, near present-day London, Ontario, Canada. Tecumseh died in the battle, and with him, his dream of an Indian confederacy.

The wider war between the United States and Great Britain continued another year. On December 24, 1814, the Treaty of Ghent formally established peace between the two nations, although the war continued in a few places until early 1815. Who won the war? It depends on who is telling the story. The war was of minor importance to the British, who were focused on Europe, not America; so they did not consider it a serious setback. The Americans celebrated withstanding British attack, an important achievement for the young nation. The Canadians claimed victory since they had not lost any land to the United States. The only clear losers were the Indians of the Old Northwest Territory, who had lost the fight for their remaining land.

The Battle of Mississinewa

When Harrison took command of the Army of the Northwest in September 1812, the war was not going well for America. The forts at Michilimackinac, Chicago, and Detroit had fallen; Fort Harrison and Fort Wayne had been attacked. An expensive war was not popular with citizens in the eastern part of the nation who no longer feared Indian violence.

In late October Harrison asked Secretary of War William Eustis for approval to attack the Miami villages on the Mississinewa River. He wrote, "Nothing can be more easy than to surprise the Miami Town of Mississineway with mounted men." He hoped a quick victory would boost support for the war. He also thought that destroying the Miami villages would prevent Indian raids on his supply lines in western Ohio. He wanted to wipe out the threat to his rear before advancing to Detroit.

Since signing the Treaty of Greenville, the Miami had kept their promise to keep the peace. Little Turtle had deterred most of his warriors from following Tecumseh and the Prophet. But Little Turtle was dead, and some Miami had joined the assaults on Fort Harrison and Fort Wayne. Harrison decided to burn the Miami villages along the Mississinewa River, where hostile warriors might gather.

Harrison chose Lieutenant Colonel John B. Campbell to command the expedition. In orders to Campbell, Harrison named Miami leaders who had "exerted themselves to keep their warriors quiet, to preserve their friendly relations with us." Among them were Pacanne, Jean Baptiste Richardville, and the brothers and sons of Little Turtle. Harrison asked that they not be harmed. He also ordered Campbell to take Indian women and children to safety at Piqua, Ohio, after their capture.

Harrison selected trader William Conner to guide the army. Conner was married to the daughter of Chief Anderson, a friendly Delaware, and familiar with the area. In preparation he marked an eighty-mile trail from Fort Greenville to the Mississinewa River.

On December 14, 1812, six hundred mounted troops began their march. The air was cold and snow was knee-deep. Harrison hoped that the Miami would be surprised by a strike in such bitter weather. The men carried only their weapons, their blankets, and three days of rations so they could move rapidly.

To avoid detection they marched straight through the night of December 16. However, as they neared the first village, scouts feared that they had been discovered. Hoping to maintain an element of surprise, Campbell ordered a quick charge. But some of his men raised such a yell that half the town's warriors escaped across the river before the army reached them. The troops shot and scalped the rest of the warriors and took forty-two prisoners. Thirty-four of the captives were women and children. All of those killed or captured belonged to the Delaware tribe, which was unquestionably loyal to the American government.

The Americans set ten of the town's twelve huts afire, with two spared to hold the prisoners. While some men stayed to guard and make camp, the rest continued down the river. They entered three more Indian towns, all deserted. But the capture of forty ponies raised the troops' spirits. After burning buildings and killing livestock, they returned to camp for the night.

Meanwhile, angry Miami warriors met to plan a course of action. From their point of view the Americans had attacked without provocation. They had butchered eight warriors, captured many innocent women and children, and burned their huts and food stores.

After the Treaty of Greenville many Miami had retreated to the Mississinewa River to escape the reach of white men, hoping to avoid more war. But once again war had found them. They could not allow the army to continue its path of destruction. They had to defend their homes.

Two hundred Miami warriors set out to attack Campbell's troops before daylight the next morning. Before the assault on their villages, most had been friendly to the American government. Among the warriors' leaders were Joseph Richardville, son of Chief Jean Baptiste Richardville, and Little Thunder, a nephew of Little Turtle.

Campbell's camp was on a bluff above the river, surrounded by dense forest on three sides. Within the camp the hungry soldiers devoured a meal of beef, obtained from slaughtered cattle. When one of the captives reported that Tecumseh and five hundred warriors were less than twenty miles away, Campbell decided to return to Greenville the next morning. His troops had suffered from frostbite, and their rations were exhausted.

About a half hour before dawn the Miami warriors began their attack. Nathaniel Vernon, of the Pittsburgh Blues, reported, "A yell pervaded the forest as if all the fiends of the lower regions had been loosed upon us." The warriors advanced to within yards of Campbell's lines. Bullets flew wildly in the dark for nearly an hour.

With daylight the Americans' aim improved, causing the Miami to withdraw. About fifty of the two hundred warriors were dead. Though only twelve of Campbell's men died that morning, forty-eight more were wounded. In addition, more than a hundred horses fell. Their bones marked the site of the battle for years to come.

The long march back to Fort Greenville took the greatest toll. Soldiers and prisoners alike suffered from hunger, fatigue, freezing temperatures, and blinding snow. Half the men were disabled by frostbite. Yet at Campbell's command the women and children rode the Indian ponies while his men trudged through the snow.

Though this is commonly viewed as a humane act in the midst of war, some soldiers resented Campbell's order. William B. Northcutt, of the Kentucky Light Dragoons, wrote, "The Commander Ordered the Indian ponies that we had caught on the 17th in the lower town be given up for the Squaws and papooses to ride, which occasioned some hard swearing amongst the Boys that Claimed them as Captured property." After seven grueling days the army arrived at Fort Greenville on Christmas Eve. Northcutt reported, "We Encamped at one Edge of the fort without putting out a regular guard and had a real old fashioned Christmas frolick."

Though the troops never reached the Miami towns at the mouth of the Mississinewa River and half the men were disabled from duty, Harrison declared the campaign a success. As he hoped, the Mississinewa valley never served as a staging ground for raids on his supply lines. However, it is likely

A sculpture portraying Colonel John B. Campbell's troops escorting captive Indian women and children through the snow following the Battle of Mississinewa. The sculpture is located on the banks of the Mississinewa River in Marion, Indiana.

that the expedition encouraged more warriors to join Tecumseh, and a desire for revenge may have fueled the Indian slaughter of wounded Americans at the River Raisin the next month.

Like Harrison, the Miami warriors of the Mississinewa River achieved their immediate goal, though at the price of many casualties. They stopped the American army's progress, leaving their villages down the river unharmed.

After the war they suffered the consequence of Harrison's ultimate victory. Along with all the tribes they were forced to sign treaties that seized more of their remaining land.

(Top and above) Every year the Mississinewa Battlefield Society hosts a reenactment of the 1812 battle.

12

William Conner (1777–1855)

I am William Conner. I live in Noblesville, Indiana, a short journey from our busy state capital. Times have changed since I first entered the territory. Now my friends and neighbors are white men like me. We live in handsome homes and dine with fine linens and silver. For almost twenty years, however, I was the only white man for miles around. I exchanged the tools of white civilization for furs the Indians brought me.

I came to the White River in the winter of 1801. My brother, John, and I worked for a French Canadian trader but soon began our own business. I traded with the Indians who lived near the White River, and John traded near a white settlement in the Whitewater Valley. I sent John pelts and skins, and he sent me the goods and whiskey desired by the Indians.

With my Indian wife and children I lived in a cabin that served as my post. My wife was Mekinges; she was the beautiful daughter of a nearby Delaware chief known as Chief Anderson. He had taken that name from his father, a white man like me who had married a Delaware woman. With our marriage I gained the friendship of her father and his Delaware tribesmen. Before long I had four sons and two daughters. My family and business prospered. I was a lucky man! In our home we spoke a Delaware dialect and lived as Indians. My Delaware neighbors treated me as one of their own. It was a comfortable life for me for I had always lived among Indians.

My father entered the Ohio wilderness decades before. Like me he sought furs and adventure. Deep in Indian country he came upon my mother, Margaret Boyer. She was a young white woman living as a Shawnee. She and her sister had been captured as children, and her sister had married a chief. The Shawnee allowed my father to marry my mother for a ransom of two hundred dollars and the promise to give up their firstborn son.

As agreed, when my brother was born, he was left with the tribe. My father bought him back when he was five. After the Moravian missionaries established Schoenbrunn my parents joined their flock. I was born there in 1777.

William Conner.

My brothers and I were the only white children in the community. My mother spoke Shawnee, our neighbors spoke Delaware, and the missionaries spoke English. I became fluent in all three languages.

I remember little of our years at Schoenbrunn since I was only four when we were forced from our village. We were marched northward by Indian allies of the British, who believed the Moravians were aiding the Americans. My family was more fortunate than most of the captives. We survived the harsh winter and were not among those who returned to Gnadenhutten to harvest the crops. But many of our neighbors were. Visions of their brutal deaths at the hands of crazed white men haunted my childhood dreams (see Chapter 1).

By the spring of 1783 my family had settled in a new Moravian settlement twenty miles from Detroit. I was six years old. When the Moravians moved on to Canada a few years later my father decided to stay. From that time on our only neighbors were Chippewa. Until 1819, when the first white settlers claimed land near my White River post, I had only lived among Indians. My fortune had been joined with theirs since birth. But the course of my life was fated to change because I was a white man.

After ceding their Ohio lands at Greenville, many Delaware had established villages beyond the treaty line along the White River (see Chapter 7). Following the Delaware were Moravian missionaries and their converts, among them Joshua Jr. I recalled him from my earliest days in Ohio. Also nearby was a band of Shawnees led by Tecumseh. His brother, Lalawethika (Tenskwatawa), resided there, too. He became known as the Prophet. These were my neighbors during my first years in Indiana.

In 1806 the Prophet called for the execution of several Indians from the White River villages. The condemned included my friend Joshua and Tedpachsit, a wise and elderly chief. They had been marked for death by their goodwill toward Americans. During my life I had been no stranger to atrocities committed by both whites and Indians. Yet this calculated killing of innocents aroused in me strong feelings of revulsion.

From that time on the Prophet's influence grew, as did my sympathy with my own race. Though I maintained great affection for my Indian family and friends, I felt more and more estranged from them. I was among the Indians, yet I was not one of them.

My brother John carried news of the Prophet to Governor William Henry Harrison. As the Prophet attracted more followers, I tried to dissuade my neighbors from joining him. Fortunately Chief Anderson was a sensible man. He knew that trouble with the Americans could only hurt his tribe. As the War of 1812 began, many Indians allied themselves with the British, but the Delaware remained neutral.

I left home to join the Americans, leaving Mekinges and my children in the care of her father. My knowledge of Indian country made me a valuable scout and guide. I hoped that after the war my service to the government would profit my family.

As the war progressed I fought in three large battles. In December 1812 I led American troops to the Mississinewa River against the Miami. The fighting was fierce. When my horse was shot down from under me I barely escaped with my life. Before we retreated we had killed forty warriors and taken as many prisoners. Unfortunately our captives were Delaware, mostly women and children. The sight of them put me in mind of my family, and I saw to their safety the best that I could.

In May 1813 I fought at Fort Meigs and in October at the Battle of the Thames. After the battle I was asked to identify the corpse of Tecumseh. While I celebrated the American victory I did not relish my special duty. In earlier years Tecumseh had been my neighbor, and I had thought him an honorable man. He had sought justice for the Indians and fought to hold their land. I now knew the land was destined for the advance of white civilization. The Indians' day was almost done.

I turned homeward, anxious for the well-being of my wife and children. Chief Anderson had followed Harrison's request to take his band to Ohio, out of the path of the army. My friends and family were safe, but the army had burned the White River towns to the ground.

I was fortunate. My trading post was unharmed, and I resumed my life as a trader. Again my home was a gathering place for the Indians and a stop on the trail for occasional white travelers. The building had two rooms, one for my stock and the other for my growing family. I was glad to be home with my wife and children. My oldest son, John, stuck to me like a shadow, learning the business of trade.

Because of my fluency in Indian languages I was paid to assist at treaty negotiations. I went to Greenville, Ohio, in July 1814 and watched my father-in-law sign for the Delaware. The treaty was called "A Treaty of Peace and Friendship," and it required the Wyandot, the Shawnee, the Delaware, the Seneca, and the Miami tribes to make peace with America and to aid in its defeat of the British. It also prohibited these tribes from making peace with any other tribe fighting against America. There seemed no need for Chief Anderson's mark because his friendship had never wavered.

My brother still did business in the growing white settlements. He was respected by all who knew him, and when Indiana achieved statehood in 1816 he became a state senator. From him I learned of ambitious plans for building highways, forming new counties, and enforcing the law. It was exciting.

In 1818 I was called to Saint Marys, Ohio, to help broker another treaty. Since the end of the war I had come to believe that the Indians' best path led to the West, away from the press of white settlement. I knew the Americans desired the Delaware country and would not stop until they owned it. As I headed to Saint Marys, I was determined to bargain well for Chief Anderson and his people. I wanted to make sure they got an ample return for their land.

My efforts paid off; the Delaware received generous terms. In exchange for their land they were given a large tract of land west of the Mississippi

River. They were given three years to prepare for their journey and would
be well-supplied with horses and food. Their debts would be fully paid, and
they would receive an annuity of four thousand dollars. At this meeting I
also secured my family's future. Knowing William Wells's Indian children
had been granted sections of land, I obtained a promise of land for my own.
I thought it was a fair agreement, and I urged Chief Anderson to sign it.

Two years later in 1820 commissioners met at my cabin to select the site
for the new state capital. It was to be located near the center of the state on
land ceded at Saint Marys. The governor of Indiana was among the guests
at my humble home. It was an honor to host such an important meeting.
The site chosen for the capital was at the junction of the White River and
Fall Creek, only twenty miles from my post. This place in the wilderness
soon would be swarming with people, and the chance for profit would be
immense. I felt the same sense of adventure as when I had come to the territory two decades before. It was as if my life were beginning anew.

Following the commissioners' visit the Indians began preparing for their
long journey west. I asked Mekinges to stay, but she chose to leave with her
father. Some wondered how I could let her go, taking our children with her.
The answer was simple. My wife and my children were Delaware. White life
would not suit them, and among the new settlers they would be subject to
scorn. I did not want that for them.

Why did I choose not to follow them west? Though I loved my family,
this place was my home. I had spent twenty years establishing myself on
this ground. I had built a fair business and looked toward exciting new
prospects. I felt called to turn forest into farmland and plant the seeds of
American culture. My past had been with the Indians, but my future was in
the new state of Indiana.

On the day of my family's removal my heart was heavy. Yet my resolve
to remain was firm. Chief Anderson took his place at the head of the line
and headed west toward the promised land. I sent sixty horses and a large
supply of goods with my wife and children. My partner, William Marshall,
chose to leave with his Delaware wife and promised to look after my family.
Parting was not easy, especially for my young children, so I rode a day with
the caravan before returning alone to my cabin.

That was the end of my life among the Indians. In my new life I have a
faithful wife, many children, and good fortune. I am surrounded by all the
comforts a man could desire. Sometimes I think of my days at the post with
Mekinges and cherish those memories. I am a lucky man, doubly blessed
with two rich and rewarding lives.

~ William Conner (1850)

Less than three months after his Delaware family's departure, William
Conner married eighteen-year-old Elizabeth Chapman, a young white woman.
They raised ten children. In 1823 he built a fine brick home for his new wife
and family, a half mile south of his post. They lived there fourteen years until
he built another house in nearby Noblesville, the county seat, which he and his
partner had platted.

Conner's fortune grew as fast as his new family. He purchased large tracts
of land with money he made from selling supplies for the Delaware removal.
At one time he held 4,000 acres in Hamilton County alone. Conner enjoyed
farming, but he also owned a distillery, mills, and other stores and businesses.
He continued to aid the American government in treaty negotiations. He was
one of the most respected men in the state, and he served three times in the
Indiana legislature.

In 1855 Conner died a wealthy man. He left a large estate and no final
will, which meant that the ownership of his property was hotly contested. His
Delaware children sued for title to the land where they had lived with him and
Mekinges, but the courts rejected their claims. His white children and their
families resided there until 1871. The property is now an interactive history
park called Conner Prairie, which depicts life in nineteenth-century Indiana.

The Fall Creek Massacre

In 1824 Conner set out with Indian Agent John Johnston on an important mission. They traveled the muddy spring trails, hoping to prevent an
outbreak of Indian violence. Moving from camp to camp they distributed gifts
of goodwill, along with pleas for patience.

They had good reason to fear unrest in the Indian camps because on
March 22, 1824, a group of white men had brutally murdered nine Indians.
Among the dead were two men, three women, and four children. Four white
men waited trial for their murder in a log jail at Pendleton, Indiana. Conner
and Johnston begged the Indians to give American justice a chance before
avenging the killings with more of the same.

The victims had built a winter camp for hunting and making maple sugar.
Their presence alarmed white settlers. Many settlers remembered past Indian
attacks on relatives and friends, and they looked upon all Indians with fear
and hatred.

Yet the vicious killings provoked disgust in the majority of citizens. They
could not condone murder, especially of innocent children. Fearing Indian

The house William Conner built in 1823 for his second wife, Elizabeth Chapman.

revenge, many fled their farms for safety in Pendleton. They anxiously awaited the trials. Like Conner and Johnston, they hoped execution of the accused would pacify the Indians. To help assure justice was done, U.S. Senator James Noble was appointed special prosecutor. He was widely known for his way with words and skill at working a jury's emotions.

However, some citizens sympathized with the prisoners and hired a team of noted defense attorneys. They viewed the crime as rightful retaliation for past Indian attacks and a way to scare Indians away from their settlement. With this attitude white men had taken Indian lives for years without legal penalty.

The trials attracted much attention across the nation. As expected, the defense rested on an age-old list of Indian offenses from burning settlers' cabins to destroying General Arthur St. Clair's army. The prosecution stressed the jurors' duty of seeing justice done, as well as avoiding Indian revenge.

In the end all four prisoners were sentenced to hang. The first, James Hudson, died on the gallows by the Pendleton Falls on January 12, 1825. The trials of Andrew Sawyer, John Bridge Sr., and John Bridge Jr. were delayed until May. Because of the younger Bridge's age, many citizens supported a petition for his pardon. Conner was one of the petitioners.

On June 3, thousands watched as the three men prepared to die. The two older men were executed promptly. They were left hanging while authorities waited to see if a last-minute pardon would arrive for the younger man. Finally the hangman could wait no longer. The young man stood, and a hood was readied to be drawn over his head. Suddenly a man on horseback galloped to the gallows. He dismounted and faced the prisoner. With great showmanship he announced, "There are sir, but two beings in this great universe who can save you from death; one is the great God of Heaven, and the other is James Brown Ray, governor of Indiana, who now stands before you. Here is your pardon. Go, sir, and sin no more!"

The crowd cheered and applauded the governor. Even the Indians appeared to approve his act of mercy. Years later a marker was placed by the falls. It reads, "Three white men were hung here in 1825 for killing Indians," commemorating the first time that white Americans were tried, convicted, and executed for the murder of Indians.

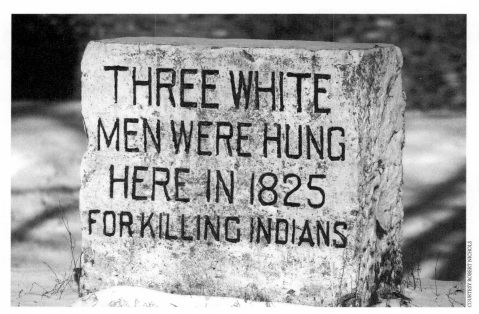

This marker is set on the location where three white men were hanged for killing Indians in Madison County, Indiana.

13

The Black Hawk War (1832)

In the early fall of 1804 four young men of the Sauk tribe, a tribe centered along the upper Mississippi River in present-day western Illinois, killed three white hunters along the Cuivre River. Hoping to avoid white revenge, the Sauk chiefs quickly admitted the warriors' guilt. They also offered gifts to compensate the families of the victims, as was their custom.

American authorities demanded that the tribe turn over the guilty warriors and asked the chiefs to meet Governor William Henry Harrison near Saint Louis. The Sauk leaders sent a delegation of five village chiefs and one of the guilty men. The warrior was immediately thrown into prison. In talks with Harrison the chiefs tried to gain their tribesman's freedom, as well as establish peaceful relations.

When the meeting ended the five chiefs returned home wearing new coats and medals. They thought that they had achieved both peace and their warrior's release by signing the papers Harrison gave them. In reality, the Treaty of Saint Louis ceded all Sauk and Fox land east of the Mississippi River to the U.S. government (see Chapter 7). The young warrior also remained in jail.

The Indians had not understood the terms of the treaty. They were unfamiliar with the American concept of individual landownership, and alcohol supplied by their hosts further clouded their understanding. The village chiefs thought they had merely accepted American rule just as they had accepted British, Spanish, and French rule in the past. They did not know that accepting American rule meant they had given away their land.

Harrison was proud of his easy acquisition, but his deceptive dealing fueled Sauk resentment for years to come. Not only were the chiefs present at the Treaty of Saint Louis unauthorized to sell land, but also a tribal council was never called to approve the treaty that ceded 51 million acres of Sauk and

Fox land. Because of the way the treaty signing was conducted, many Sauk, such as war leader Black Hawk, refused to accept its validity.

As more land opened for settlement, pioneers poured into Indiana and Illinois to farm the rich soil. In 1800 the white population of the area was fewer than 6,000. However, by 1830 there were nearly 500,000 whites in the Indiana/Illinois region. As settlers filled the grounds the Indians lived and hunted in, the Sauk were forced farther west to hunt. The land to the west was not empty, of course, so the Sauk came into conflict with the Sioux Indians.

The interests of Indians were often at odds with those of their white neighbors. One dispute occurred between settler William Davis and nearby Potawatomi tribesmen. Davis had dammed Indian Creek in western Illinois in order to build a sawmill. However, the dam blocked fish from reaching the Indian village, which decreased the villagers' food supply. When Davis ignored Indian complaints, a young warrior tried to tear down the dam, but Davis caught and beat him.

To eliminate such conflicts, the Illinois governor demanded that the federal government remove the tribes from the state. In the summer of 1828 federal officials told Sauk chiefs to move their villages west of the Mississippi River. The Sauk protested that they had never ceded their land to the United States because the Treaty of Saint Louis was invalid.

While on his winter hunt in 1829, Sauk war leader Black Hawk learned that white squatters had moved into his Rock River village. When he went to investigate, he found his own dwelling occupied. He asked authorities to evict the squatters, and since the government had not yet sold this piece of land, his complaint was valid. Yet the American government disregarded Black Hawk's complaint. He was advised to make a new home west of the Mississippi River because the government would sell the land to settlers the next fall.

Despite that advice Black Hawk brought his band back to the Rock River valley to plant their crops. He returned the next two years and occupied land not yet farmed by the settlers. Frightened by the Indians' presence, the settlers demanded the Indians' eviction. On June 3, 1831, General Edmund Gaines called the Sauk leaders to meet him at nearby Fort Armstrong. Facing Gaines, Black Hawk asserted that his people only wished to harvest their corn and would stay to do so. But when a large army arrived, Black Hawk yielded to government demands. The Sauk chiefs signed a peace document, promising to stay west of the Mississippi River.

INDIANA HISTORICAL SOCIETY

Portrait of Black Hawk, painted by James Otto Lewis, circa 1830s.

It appeared that Black Hawk, nearly sixty-five years old, had finally accepted the necessity of going west. The aging warrior settled his band along the banks of the Iowa River. His followers included militant Sauk, as well as members of other tribes who resisted adapting to white culture. However, it was not long before the old warrior's desire to return to the Rock River was revived. Napope, a young Sauk chief, brought news from Fort Malden. He said British authorities would help Black Hawk fight the Americans.

White Cloud, a Winnebago Indian prophet, also raised Black Hawk's hopes. Like the Shawnee Prophet before him, White Cloud preached a return to traditional Indian ways. Black Hawk valued his visions and guidance. That winter White Cloud invited Black Hawk to bring his band to White Cloud's village on the Rock River. He said that Black Hawk would receive aid from the Winnebago, Potawatomi, and Ottawa tribes, as well as from the British. White Cloud foresaw that all the Indians would join him in war by autumn.

Encouraged by Napope and White Cloud, Black Hawk and his followers crossed the Mississippi River on April 5, 1832. One thousand men, women, and children made their way toward White Cloud's village. On April 16 Governor John Reynolds sounded the alarm to the citizens of Illinois, announcing, "The Indians . . . have invaded the State. . . . I consider the settlers on the frontier in imminent danger." His dramatic announcement created hysteria.

U.S. Army general Henry Atkinson was concerned but did not believe that war was imminent. Since Black Hawk was traveling with women and children, Atkinson did not think Black Hawk planned to fight soon. Atkinson urged the governor to avoid provoking hostilities. Instead, he urged the governor to construct a thought-out plan. He believed the Indians could be turned back without bloodshed, as they had been the previous summer. Reynolds would not be deterred. Hoping to impress the voters of Illinois, he sprang into action and immediately authorized Major Isaiah Stillman to raise a militia to confront Black Hawk's band and force them from Illinois. Meanwhile, Black Hawk was meeting with Winnebago, Potawatomi, and Ottawa leaders. To his dismay he found that they had no intention of supplying him with either food or warriors, and there would be no help from the British. Black Hawk realized Napope's words were lies and White Cloud's prophecies wishful thinking. Soon a messenger came to warn him that a thousand mounted white men were moving up the Rock River. Black Hawk had only a few hundred warriors to protect many women and children. He knew he must retreat once more across the Mississippi River.

On May 14 Stillman's raw recruits camped near Black Hawk's band. Wishing to negotiate a safe return to Iowa, Black Hawk sent three warriors with a white flag to the camp and three others to watch at a distance. However, Stillman had no interpreter, and many of his men had been drinking. When the Indians approached, the camp erupted in chaos. Stillman's men killed one of the flag bearers and two of the watchers. The three surviving warriors rushed back to Black Hawk with the militia in close pursuit.

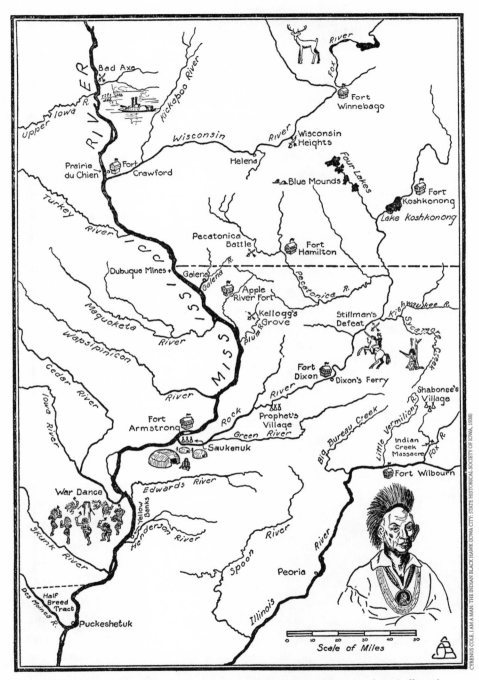

Bad Axe

RIVER

Upper Iowa R.

Kickapoo River

River

Fort Winnebago

Wisconsin River

Wisconsin Heights

Prairie du Chien

Fort Crawford

Helena

Blue Mounds

Four Lakes

Fort Koshkonong

Lake Koshkonong

Turkey River

Pecatonica Battle

Fort Hamilton

Dubuque Mines

Galena

Galena R.

Pecatonica R.

Apple River Fort

Maquoketa River

Wapsipinicon River

Kellogg's Grove

Stillman's Defeat

Kishwaukee R.

Sycamore Creek

Cedar River

Plum

Fort Dixon

Dixon's Ferry

Shabonee's Village

Iowa River

Fort Armstrong

Rock River

Prophet's Village

Green River

Big Bureau Creek

Little Vermilion

Indian Creek Massacre

FOX

Saukenuk

Fort Wilbourn

War Dance

Edwards River

Yellow Banks

Henderson River

Spoon River

River

Illinois River

Peoria

Skunk River

Des Moines R.

Half Breed Tract

Puckeshetuk

MISSISSIPPI

Scale of Miles

0 10 20 30 40 50

A map illustrating the important sites related to the Black Hawk War, such as Stillman's Defeat, the Battle of Wisconsin Heights, and the Battle of Bad Axe.

Though most of his men were hunting, Black Hawk chose to stay and fight. He ordered his warriors to form a line behind a row of bushes. When the white men drew near, the Indians charged with a volley of gunfire.

The white militiamen greatly outnumbered the Indians, but the Indians' charge terrified them so much that they ran for their lives. In remembrance of their flight, the brief skirmish became known as the Battle of Stillman's Run. Three Indians and eleven militiamen were killed, but with each retelling the size of the battle grew. This battle marks the beginning of the Black Hawk War.

The rest of the war was as senseless as its beginning. Black Hawk led his band north, trying to evade the Americans while seeking a safe chance to cross the Mississippi River. Along the way up the river, the Indians attacked settlements using guerrilla warfare. Elsewhere, isolated incidents of violence broke out, unrelated to Black Hawk's band. Some Indians used the unrest to settle old scores. The most deadly attack was known as the Indian Creek Massacre. In this act of revenge, Potawatomi warriors raided the farm of Davis—the man who had built the dam impeding their fishing. They killed fifteen settlers and took two captives. When word of the massacre spread, more settlers fled from the fields to the towns. This included militiamen. One brigade had advanced to the site of Stillman's Run. Alarmed at the sight of their dead comrades, the men rushed to the town of Ottawa to be discharged.

Engraving by Henry Lewis depicting the American steamship, Warrior, *firing upon Indians at the Battle of Bad Axe in August 1832.*

President Andrew Jackson ordered eight hundred troops to Illinois under the command of General Winfield Scott. They boarded ships in Buffalo, New York, and steamed across the Great Lakes to Chicago, but cholera broke out among the soldiers. By the time the ships docked in Chicago, fewer than two hundred men were fit to fight. In the end, cholera proved more deadly to white citizens than the warring Indians.

The militia caught up with Black Hawk's band on July 21 at the Wisconsin River. A true battle—the Battle of Wisconsin Heights—was fought, and nearly seventy Indians died before crossing. Again the Indians tried to surrender, but communication failed and the chase continued.

Black Hawk's band, reduced to only five hundred men, women, and children, finally reached the Mississippi River on August 1. As the Indians rushed to build rafts, the American steamship *Warrior* came into view. Black Hawk raised a white flag and waded toward the warship. But once again communications failed, and the ship opened fire on the Indians. Two dozen warriors died before it steamed away to refuel. This became known as the Battle of Bad Axe.

That night Black Hawk urged his followers to abandon the immediate plan to cross the river. He advised them to follow him farther north instead, but most of them refused. The next morning American troops arrived, trapping the Indians on the riverbank. Desperate mothers plunged into the water with children on their backs.

The *Warrior* reappeared and fired its cannon. For eight hours Americans troops fired at the men, women, and children cowering on the riverbank and swimming in the water. Few of Black Hawk's followers escaped death that day, and those who did reach the river's west shore were hunted down by enemy Sioux, who presented their scalps to a government agent. This slaughter of women and children was one of the worst tragedies in American history.

Black Hawk finally surrendered on August 27. Along with White Cloud and Napope he was imprisoned in Saint Louis. The prisoners were sent to Washington, DC, the following spring. On June 5 they were released and carried home along a winding route. In the cities of the East they were greeted as folk heroes. Large crowds cheered the Indians who had dared to challenge white authority. In the West, where citizens still feared Indian attack, they were viewed with more suspicion.

The Black Hawk War resulted in fewer than seventy white deaths, including soldiers and civilians, and it was estimated that several hundred Indians died. In the end, the war served as an excuse for another round of treaties that required Indians to relinquish their lands. Even tribes who had remained loyal to the United States were forced to surrender large tracts of land. By 1842 the government had purchased all Indian land in Iowa. The westward expansion of white civilization could not be impeded.

Chief Leopold Pokagon

Alarmed by the war in neighboring Illinois, Indiana settlers sent a delegation to determine the intentions of Potawatomi chief Leopold Pokagon. Pokagon's band lived near present-day South Bend, Indiana. Pokagon stated that he would remain neutral. But his pledge of peace did not calm white fears. On hearing news of Pokagon's words, one excited man cried, "That damn neutral is now not twenty miles from here!"

The settlers had no reason to fear Pokagon, who had always sought peace. According to his son, the chief had tried to stop the Fort Dearborn massacre, which occurred in August 1812. The massacre took place less than two miles from Fort Dearborn (present-day Chicago) when approximately five hundred Potawatomi attacked the men, women, and children who had been ordered to evacuate the fort and head to safety in Detroit. Fifty-two people were killed in the massacre. Instead, Pokagon had encouraged his tribesmen to adopt many of their white neighbors' ways. In turn, he hoped his neighbors would allow his band to remain in northern Indiana.

When President Jackson signed the Indian Removal Act in 1830, Pokagon visited Father Gabriel Richard in Detroit. He asked that the "black robes" be sent to his village. Pokagon believed the Catholic Church would be a valuable ally in his quest to avoid removal.

In response to Pokagon's request, Father Stephen Badin was sent to the Saint Joseph valley, where he formally baptized the Indians of Pokagon's band. In 1831 Badin built a log chapel on Lake Saint Mary, where the University of Notre Dame was later established.

In 1833, after the Black Hawk War, the Potawatomi chiefs were called to Fort Dearborn to negotiate a new treaty. The treaty ceded their remaining land in northern Indiana, as well as tracts in present-day Michigan, Illinois, and Wisconsin. The treaty also required their removal to land west of the Mississippi River, but Pokagon was determined to stay on the land of his ancestors. During negotiations he spoke of his people's friendship with the government, their conversion to Catholicism, and their move toward individual landownership. His words convinced the commissioners to exempt his band from

Chief Leopold Pokagon.

removal. A few years later he used treaty money to buy 840 acres in nearby Michigan, of which he gave forty acres to the Catholic Church for a church and school.

Yet Pokagon's struggle was not over. In 1840 Secretary of War Joel R. Poinsett ordered General Hugh Brady to remove all remaining Potawatomi from Indiana and Michigan. Pokagon went to court to protest. A judge of the Michigan Supreme Court ruled in Pokagon's favor and agreed that removal of Pokagon's band would violate the 1833 treaty.

Pokagon presented the court document to Brady. The general issued a pass ensuring the band's right to live there undisturbed. Pokagon had saved the land for his people. This was a remarkable achievement in the midst of the government's determined program of Indian removal. When Pokagon died in 1841 he was buried at the church on the land he had provided. As he wished, his bones and those of his followers remained on the ground of their ancestors.

14

Maconaquah (1773–1847)

My white sister puts all my words on paper for remembering. But for the Indian, there is no need for paper. Our history stays always in our thoughts, ready for the telling. I remember all my life as an Indian, though my days as a white child have passed away like mounds of melting snow. When I became an Indian, I forgot all my white ways and words.

My white sister and brothers want me to recall my life with them. They say they have searched for me for sixty years. I believe their words. I can see their faces on my daughters and grandchildren. But they lost a small white girl with hair like flames. I am an old Indian woman with hair of spent embers.

I close my eyes and my mind tries to see for them. I see a man in a big hat and dark coat. They say this man was my father, and our family was Quaker. My sister calls me Frances, and there is a small stirring in my heart. Yes, I was once Frances Slocum.

I was the girl hiding under the stairs as warriors burst into the cabin. My brother was with me. The Indians threw us over their shoulders and raced toward the woods. My mother sprang from the bushes to stop them. "The boy is lame!" she shouted. They dropped my brother but ran on with me. I cried as my mother's voice got fainter and fainter.

My father had said the Indians were our friends. I held his words in my heart. When we stopped to sleep, the Indians gave me food and wrapped me in a soft skin. My father was right. I thanked my new friends for their gifts. This seemed to please them very much.

My sister asks how I fared with the Indians. Was I well cared for? Was I happy? Yes and yes! I was always treated with kindness. I became the daughter of a Delaware chief called Tuckhorse and his wife, Sheekee. I took the place of their dead daughter. They gave me their daughter's name, Sheletawash, and raised me as their own. All they had was offered to me. My days were full of their devotion.

Frances Slocum.

We stayed our first winter by the great falls. The British fort was there. The Redcoats were at war with the Long Knives. They gave us food and protected us from the Long Knives.

After the snows melted, we were always traveling. We moved along the south shore of the lake to the Delaware villages of the Ohio Country. Tuckhorse spoke with the chiefs about making war on the Long Knives. He said they were taking our land, and we must help their British fathers fight them. Captain Pipe agreed, but other chiefs did not. They said the Long Knives would win the war, so Indians must keep their friendship.

When leaves fell from the trees, we returned to the Niagara. Then after another winter we journeyed along the lake's north shore. We finally reached the fort at Detroit. Many warriors brought scalps to the British father there. At first their gifts repulsed me, but they were at war with men who had stolen their land and murdered their wives and children. To stop all the killing, they had to ignite fear in the hearts of the Long Knives.

We lived near Detroit for three years. My father built chairs, and my mother and I made brooms and baskets. We sold them at the fort. Our work brought us a comfortable dwelling and plenty of food for our bellies.

During this time I heard of the massacre at Gnadenhutten (see Chapter 1). One hundred peaceful Indians were murdered by savage white men. On learning this, I grew ashamed of my white skin. My greatest fear was being torn from my Delaware family.

When the Long Knives' war with the Redcoats ended, I went with my parents to Kekionga. The Miami allowed us to live there. Kekionga was at the headwaters of the Maumee River, west of the Great Black Swamp. My father hoped that hidden deep in Indian territory I would never be forced to return to the white world.

My sister asks of my marriage and children. I married twice. My first husband was not good, so I returned to my parents. The next was an honorable Miami man who cared for me and our children well. His name was Shapoconah. When I joined him as a Miami, I was named Maconaquah, which means Little Bear Woman.

I found Shapoconah after the Indians fought Anthony Wayne at Fallen Timbers. I had gone with my parents near the site of the battle. There, a warrior was waiting to die inside a hollow log. It was Shapoconah.

With my parents I cared for his wounds and brought back his health. He returned our help by bringing us meat the next winter. We were fortunate. Many Indians were starving because the Long Knives had burnt our crops. I began to love this brave and kind man, and he loved me.

For the first years of our marriage we stayed near Kekionga, but we finally moved down the Mississinewa River, far from the American fort. There were many Miami villages there. Most of our days were happy. We would often join friends for feasting and games. Each summer we gathered for the Green Corn Dance. We wore our finest clothing with bells on our ankles. We danced to the beat of the drum and clatter of deer hooves. The men moved round the circle, hopping quickly from foot to foot. One by one the women took partners. The music and dancing came faster and faster. Suddenly it stopped with a sharp, loud cry of the dancers. Eeiiiii! My spirit sprang skyward in a great burst of joy.

Along with the good days came days of sorrow. We kept two daughters, but twice we buried small sons. Despite our prosperity, times were hard for the Indians. In 1812 the Long Knives invaded our ground. Shapoconah joined the warriors defending our homes. After the battle his world grew quiet, and our town became known as Deaf Man's Village.

The white men continued to take more land and emptied the forest of game. With the loss of hunting, many of our warriors had trouble finding their manhood. Some were crazy from the white man's drink. They beat their wives and killed one another.

Our older daughter, Kekenakushwa, married a good man. He is a skilled hunter and lays up corn and hay for the winter. But our younger daughter, Ozahshinquah, was not so lucky. Her first husband was a lazy drunkard, and the second died in a brawl with a Wea. She had four worthless husbands before marrying Wahpopetah Bondie. At last I may rest, knowing she will be cared for. Her new man is kind and does well for his family.

Here at Deaf Man's Village my cabin is as good as any white woman's. My daughters and grandchildren live with me. What more could an old woman want? We have six beds, many chairs, and pretty dishes for our table. Our dresses are covered with beads and silver. We have sixty strong horses, a hundred hogs, and a large herd of cattle on our farm.

My white brother asks that I join him in Pennsylvania. He means to be kind, but my home is here. Why should I leave it? The Great Spirit has always allowed me to live with the Indians, and I am used to them. Away, I would be a fish out of water.

I have but one wish. I wish to remain in Deaf Man's Village. And when it is time to go to the Spirit World, I wish my bones to rest on this ground, beside my sons and husband. Though I will not leave my home, I invite the Slocums to live here with me. I will gladly give them a share of my land. They can teach my children the best ways of farming and how to live among white men. I would happily go to the Spirit World, knowing my family will prosper at Deaf Man's Village.

~ Maconaquah (1837)

In 1840 the Miami signed a treaty agreeing to leave Indiana for a reservation in the West. Their removal came in 1846. Maconaquah's brothers successfully petitioned the U.S. government to allow her family to stay. John Quincy Adams pleaded their case, and Maconaquah's daughters were given ownership of the square mile of land surrounding Deaf Man's Village.

In 1846 a white nephew came to live near Maconaquah. She adopted him as her son. He was a devout Baptist, and along with lessons on farming he taught her sons-in-law Christianity. Both became preachers and showed their tribesmen the ways of white settlers. Maconaquah's family prospered. Her grandson, Camillus Bundy, became chief of the Miami Indians of Indiana.

Maconaquah remained with her children and grandchildren until her death in 1847. Her family, Indian and white, laid her to rest near her husband and sons. In the Miami tradition they raised a white flag so the Great Spirit could find her. No stone marked the grave, but in 1900 her Slocum relatives erected a marker to tell her story. The graves of her daughters, sons-in-law, and grandchildren still surround her.

The Search for Frances Slocum

Delaware raiders snatched five-year-old Frances Slocum from her Pennsylvania home in 1778. Her family never stopped searching for her. Fifty-nine years passed before they found her in Indiana.

Frances's parents were Quakers. Their pacifist beliefs kept them from fighting in the Revolutionary War. Hoping to distance themselves from the

George Winter, an artist in the early to mid-1800s, observed and visited Indian tribes. He sketched and painted scenes from these observations. This painting is of Deaf Man's Village, where Frances Slocum lived with her husband, Shapoconah.

war, they moved to the Wyoming valley near present-day Wilkes-Barre, Pennsylvania. But they could not escape the fighting. The Delaware had recently been forced from the valley. In anger they attacked the frontier settlement. Despite his Quaker beliefs, Frances's brother, Giles, joined in defending his neighbors.

Though many settlers fled in fear, Frances's father decided to stay. He thought the Indians knew his desire for peace. But during the fighting, they had noticed Giles's Quaker hat and marked the family for revenge. They raided the Slocum cabin and stole Frances. Six weeks later they killed Frances's father and grandfather.

Ruth Slocum never forgot her young daughter's cries as she disappeared into the forest. She was determined to find her. Over the years she and her sons took many trips to search for Frances. They interviewed traders, attended treaty negotiations, and offered large rewards for word of her.

After Ruth's death her sons continued the quest. Once they traveled to Ohio to visit a Wyandot chief who was rumored to have a white wife. But again they were disappointed because the woman was not Frances.

In 1835 a white trader named George Ewing stopped at Maconaquah's home for the night. Ewing could speak the Miami language and had been a friend of her husband. To him she revealed her lifelong secret. She was a white woman. She said her father's name was Slocum, and they had lived on the Susquehanna River.

Ewing tried to find Maconaquah's white family. He wrote a letter to the postmaster of Lancaster, Pennsylvania, and asked him to print it in the local paper. The letter was finally read by a minister who had lived in the Wyoming valley. He knew of the Slocum family's search for the lost sister and sent the letter to Frances's brother Joseph in Wilkes-Barre. Joseph wrote to his brother and sister who were living in Ohio. Though quite elderly, all three immediately set off for Indiana. Could this Indian woman be their sister?

On meeting Maconaquah they examined her left forefinger. They knew Frances's finger had been accidentally smashed by a hammer. They found the finger disfigured. Maconaquah was Frances! The Slocums could not speak with their sister without an interpreter. She feared being forced from her Indian home, so their meeting was not the joyous reunion they had long imagined. Gradually they gained Maconaquah's trust. The story of the white girl who became an Indian captured the imagination of the American public and popularized a more sympathetic view of Indian life.

The Potawatomi removal began in September and reached its terminus in November. On the 600-mile "Trail of Death" from northern Indiana to Kansas, approximately forty people died—most of whom were children. (This map was adapted from resources compiled by the Fulton County Historical Society and the Potawatomi Trail of Death Association, Rochester, Indiana, including map by Potawatomi Tom Hamilton, "Potawatomi 'Trail of Death' March: Sept.—Nov. 1838," 2004.)

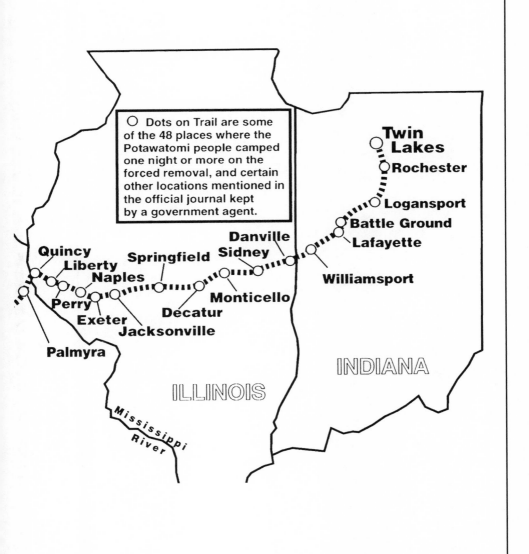

○ Dots on Trail are some of the 48 places where the Potawatomi people camped one night or more on the forced removal, and certain other locations mentioned in the official journal kept by a government agent.

Twin Lakes

Rochester

Logansport

Battle Ground

Lafayette

Danville

Sidney

Williamsport

Quincy

Liberty

Naples

Springfield

Perry

Monticello

Exeter

Decatur

Jacksonville

Palmyra

INDIANA

ILLINOIS

Mississippi River

15

The Potawatomi Trail of Death (1838)

On September 4, 1838, Potawatomi chief Menominee was forced into a jail wagon with two other chiefs. The wagon was part of a long caravan. Leading the procession were armed guards on horseback, proudly bearing an American flag. More than 800 Indians followed. As the Indians left their camp, their old homes were set on fire. By the time they reached their new reservation in Kansas, more than forty lay in unmarked graves along the way. This was the Potawatomi Trail of Death.

With the Indian Removal Act of 1830, President Andrew Jackson's agents forced the tribes to cede their lands east of the Mississippi River in exchange for lands in the West. Jackson described it as a "benevolent policy." He claimed it would "separate the Indians from immediate contact with settlements of whites" and "enable them to pursue happiness in their own way." Most Indians did not look upon it so favorably.

Menominee was a Potawatomi chief who had resisted selling his land. He and his band wished to remain in their village near present-day Plymouth, Indiana. After visiting Baptist missionary Isaac McCoy in 1821, Menominee began to preach Christianity. He urged his followers to give up strong drink, to live in peace with their neighbors, and to take up farming. He carved a notch on a pole for each of his many sermons. As his village grew from four huts to one hundred, the pole became filled with notches. A log chapel was built for services.

In the 1832 Treaty of Tippecanoe the Potawatomi ceded most of their land in northwest Indiana in exchange for $130,000 in goods and a $20,000 annuity. Smaller reservations were carved out of the ceded territory for village chiefs. Menominee was to share twenty-two sections (or square miles) of land with three other chiefs.

The American government soon pressured the chiefs to give up their reservations, but Menominee would not sign. In 1834 he invited the Catholic priests (black robes) to establish a mission in his village. The priests supported the chief's resolve to remain on his land. Because of their support, Indian Agent Abel Pepper refused the priests' request to build a school in Menominee's village.

Throughout the summer of 1836 Pepper worked unsuccessfully to complete a treaty with Menominee. Finally, he brokered a treaty with the other three chiefs for land that included Menominee's village. In this treaty the three agreed to move west of the Mississippi River within two years. But Menominee still would not sign.

Hundreds of Potawatomi flocked to Menominee's village hoping to avoid removal. Father Benjamin Petit encouraged them to petition the government to stay, but their petitions failed. Petit fumed, "It is impossible for me . . . to conceive how such events may take place in this country of liberty."

While meeting with government officials, Menominee made a fiery speech refusing to leave his land. He said that the president "would not drive me from my home and the graves of my tribe, and my children, who have gone to the Great Spirit, nor allow you to tell me that your braves will take me, tied like a dog, if he knew the truth. . . . I have not sold my lands. I will not sell them. I have not signed any treaty, and I shall not sign any. I am not going to leave my lands, and I do not want to hear anything more about it."

George Winter observed the Potawatomi Trail of Death in 1838. Winter's sketch illustrates how many people were forcibly evicted from their homes.

Anticipating the Indians' departure, white squatters moved onto Menominee's land. Violence followed. Indians damaged a squatter's cabin, and the squatters burned several Indian homes. Fearing further acts of revenge, the squatters appealed to Indiana governor David Wallace for help. Wallace ordered General John Tipton to force the Indians from their lands and begin their journey west. To carry out the plan, Pepper invited Menominee and his followers to a meeting on August 29. When they arrived, Tipton and his men seized them.

The Indians were heavily guarded. Petit and Bishop Simon Brute came to the camp and comforted the nearly 300 Indians suffering from typhoid fever. On Sunday, September 9, 1838, the priests held Mass for the departing Indians. The caravan left the next morning, and Petit accompanied them. The late summer weather was hot and dry. Fresh water was scarce, and food supplied by the traders was so poor that the guards refused to eat it. Typhoid took a heavy toll. There were deaths almost every day. When the caravan finally reached Kansas, an accounting was made. Of the 859 Potawatomi that had begun the journey only 756 completed it.

Weakened by the journey, Petit died on his way home in February 1839. Two months later Tipton died in Logansport, Indiana, at age fifty-two. Some said his death was due to an Indian curse. Menominee and his band moved on to a Kansas mission, where the chief died two years later.

By 1907 the citizens of Indiana had revised their view of Menominee. No longer fearful of Indians, they regretted the injustice done. They erected a monument honoring the chief at the site of his former village. Though Menominee's bones rest in Kansas, his likeness looks over the land he struggled so hard to hold.

The Shawnee Leave Ohio

The Shawnee were a mobile people. They had fled west and south from the Ohio valley when the Iroquois invaded in the late 1600s. Though some Shawnee returned in the 1700s, many again departed when the Americans burned their villages. The rest withdrew to the Auglaize and upper Miami Rivers in present-day northwest Ohio. Chief Black Hoof established his village there. After the American victory at Fallen Timbers, he decided his tribe's best hope for survival lay in living in harmony with the white men. He invited the Quakers to teach his tribesmen new methods of farming. During the War of 1812 he aided the American army. He was determined his followers could live in peace

with their neighbors and remain on
their land.

In 1817 Black Hoof signed the
Treaty of the Maumee Rapids. In this
treaty the Indians ceded four million
acres of northwest Ohio. But within
this area some chiefs were granted
reservations. Black Hoof received a
large tract surrounding his village of
Wapakoneta.

Despite Black Hoof's efforts,
white settlers resented the Shawnee
in their midst. The more successful
the Indians became at farming, the
more the settlers desired the land for
themselves. They trespassed on the

Black Hoof.

Indians' reservations, stole livestock, and destroyed Shawnee belongings. They
hoped their harassment would convince the Indians to move west.

In 1825 the settlers gained an unexpected ally in their campaign to
remove the Shawnee. Tenskwatawa, the Shawnee Prophet, arrived at Wapakoneta to convince his tribesmen to remove with him to the West. Since
the War of 1812 the Prophet had been an exile in Canada. But he wanted to
live again among his tribesmen. In exchange for permission to return to the
United States, he promised to persuade the Shawnee to leave Ohio. He saw his
agreement with the American government as a chance to reclaim prestige and
followers.

Perhaps the Prophet sincerely believed that his tribesmen would benefit
from moving west. He might have hoped that in the West he could return
them to traditional ways. However, Black Hoof argued that it was impossible
to escape white settlers. He knew they would enter the western territory, just
as they had come to Ohio from the East. He thought the best course of action
was to hold their Ohio ground and learn to live with their new white neighbors.

The Prophet persuaded 250 Shawnee to follow him west. In this strange
twist of events one of the fiercest advocates of the Indians' land rights brought
about their removal from that land. The Shawnee left Ohio on September
20, 1826, but the government had not planned well for their journey. Soon

they had no food, money, or guides. The Shawnee did not arrive at their new reservation in Kansas until May 14, 1828. They blamed the Prophet for their misfortunes, and he never regained his former leadership role.

Black Hoof and his remaining followers continued to stand their ground in Ohio. In 1831, near ninety years old, Black Hoof died. He was laid to rest on the land he loved. With his death the Shawnee lost a strong voice of resistance, and the American government stepped up its efforts to seize their land.

James B. Gardiner was appointed to conclude a removal treaty. He threatened the Indians with grave consequences if they remained in Ohio. He warned that white men would beat and kill tribesmen without penalty. The government would not use the laws of white citizens to protect the Indians. Gardiner's threats proved effective. The Shawnee signed a treaty ceding their remaining Ohio reservations. In return they were promised 100,000 acres west of the Mississippi River. In the fall of 1832 the Shawnee began their long trek west, and their land was sold to eager white settlers.

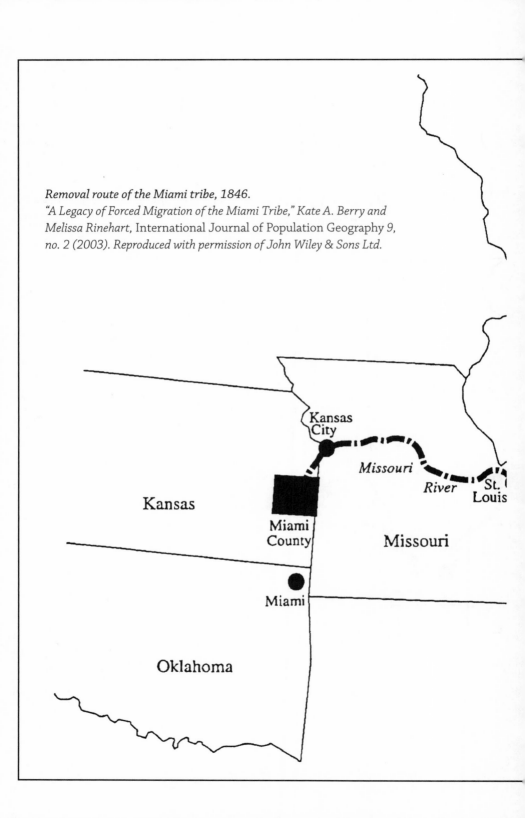

Removal route of the Miami tribe, 1846.
"A Legacy of Forced Migration of the Miami Tribe," Kate A. Berry and
Melissa Rinehart, International Journal of Population Geography 9,
no. 2 (2003). *Reproduced with permission of John Wiley & Sons Ltd.*

Kansas City

Missouri
River

St.
Louis

Kansas

Miami
County

Missouri

Miami

Oklahoma

Wisconsin

Lake
Michigan

Michigan

Illinois

Wabash Erie
Canal

Fort
Wayne

Miami
Erie
Canal

Ohio

Peru

Indiana

Dayton

Cincinnati

Mississippi
River

Ohio River

Louisville

Cairo

Kentucky

16

Chief Jean Baptiste Richardville (1761–1841)

My name is Jean Baptiste Richardville. God has granted me a long and prosperous life. My business in trade has brought me great fortune. As principal chief of the Miami, I devoted myself to the welfare of my people. Now I am an old man. Knowing the uncertainties of life, I must put my affairs, and those of my tribe, in order.

I will give my land to my children and grandchildren. Having learned the ways of white men, they may flourish among them. My bones and theirs will remain on our ancient ground. Yet I fear for our tribe's future. Every year the white men increase, while our number grows smaller. We have become strangers in the land of our birth, even to ourselves and to each other.

Once the Miami were a proud people. Our lands reached from the lakes of the north to the banks of the Ohio River. Our men were skilled hunters and warriors, and our women tended endless fields of corn. We traded with our French fathers, and we were a wealthy nation. This was the world in the days of my youth.

My family was well-known among the Miami. My father was Antoine Joseph Drouet de Richardville, a successful French trader. My mother was Tacumwah, the sister of Pacanne, who was the chief of all the Miami. We lived in his village at Kekionga. Our kinsman, Meshekinnoquah (Little Turtle), was a noted warrior.

In that time the Miami lived in harmony with our French neighbors. Friendships between us were common. My parents' marriage created a powerful partnership. My father gained support and protection from my mother's family, and my mother gained access to the European goods desired by our people. My mother became the most powerful woman in our tribal council.

The Wabash and Maumee Rivers ran through the heart of our territory. Our rivers connected Lake Erie with the Mississippi River. On these waters goods passed all the way from Upper Canada to the Gulf of Mexico. Near our home was a nine-mile stretch of land between the rivers. My family

Portrait of Chief Richardville by James Otto Lewis, 1827. He is shown wearing European-style clothing and a Jefferson Medal.

controlled this portage. We charged a toll to carry goods between the rivers and often collected a hundred dollars a day. In this way we achieved great wealth.

When my father returned to Canada, I sometimes stayed with him there. I attended school and became fluent in English and French. At my father's house I read many books, listened to music, and admired fine paintings. I lived as a white man with him. Back in Kekionga I lived as an Indian. I spoke as a Miami, learned a warrior's ways, and followed my mother in trade.

After my father left us my mother married Charles Beaubien, a trader and British agent to the Miami. He was respected by our tribe and gave us guns and powder to fight the Long Knives. Beaubien helped us defend our territory.

During those days of conflict I was tested as a warrior. I was known as Peshewa, which means the wildcat. I followed my kinsman Meshekinno-quah in war. In spite of my cautious nature I learned to be bold and decisive. The proper balance of watchfulness and action made Meshekinnoquah a great war chief.

When I was nineteen I fought my first battle. A Frenchman, Augustin Mottin de La Balme, had invaded our towns. Most of our warriors were away on the hunt, and our women and children had fled to the Eel River villages. In Kekionga La Balme's men ransacked the stores of my mother's husband, Beaubien. My mother and Beaubien asked Meshekinnoquah for help. He gathered a war party, and I was one of his warriors. But Meshek-innoquah did not strike immediately. Instead he watched and waited. He waited until our chance to defeat the invaders was greatest.

After many days of looting, La Balme left our towns and camped for the night by the Eel River. This was our chance to surprise him. When the time was right, Meshekinnoquah moved decisively. We stormed La Balme's camp before dawn, killing the greedy white men while they slept. It was a great victory. I never forgot my kinsman's lesson—watch and wait patiently, then act boldly!

Five years later I used this lesson to claim my place as the leader of all the Miami. The role was passed from the chief to a son of one of his sisters, and since my mother was a sister of Chief Pacanne I could succeed him. But Pacanne had many nephews also vying to succeed him. My ambitious mother encouraged me to win the title. Though my boyhood manner had been shy and retiring, as a man I was determined to serve my tribe and please my mother. I waited patiently for the opportunity to earn the role of chief. Finally that chance came.

One day our warriors brought a captive to our village. The forest echoed with their cries of triumph. The council decided the prisoner should burn at the stake. I had often witnessed such events. Burnings satisfied our warriors' need for revenge. One small clan of our tribe even ate their captives' charred remains. Though this practice was rare, it served the purpose of striking terror into the hearts of our enemies.

As soon as the prisoner's fate was announced, I thought carefully on what I must do. Having made my plan, I joined my mother at the back of the crowd that had gathered for the burning. Like Meshekinnoquah I watched and waited. Then, just at the right moment, when the torch touched the tinder, I sprang forward. I drew my knife and cut the white man free. There were gasps of surprise, then shouts of approval. My bold act had earned the crowd's admiration.

I had won the right to follow my uncle as chief. From that time onward I served as his deputy and learned the duties of his position. When he was away I served as village chief. In 1795 I signed for our tribe at Greenville. It was the first of many times I negotiated with the Americans. By the time of Pacanne's death I was ready to become the principal chief of the Miami.

Over time I learned the Americans' desire for land would not diminish. If we would not sell our land, they would take it. So I decided to bargain for the best possible price. With this goal I brought much gold and silver to our tribe. But with each treaty we lost more land. The Miami might be fed and clothed with annuity payments, but where would they live? Soon there would be no ground to stand on.

I knew that white men held individual plots of ground for their homes. I decided this must also be the way of the Miami. Only by owning individual plots could we expect to preserve any of our ancestors' ground. From then on I bargained for small tracts of land to be given to prominent tribesmen. In 1818, at the Treaty of Saint Marys, I received seven sections of land near Fort Wayne and two at the western end of our portage at the Forks of the Wabash. I hoped to use this land as a refuge for all the Miami.

Yet my heart was saddened by the degradation of our once proud people. They no longer heard the voices of our ancestors. Unmarried women were having children. Couples were marrying before reaching maturity. When drinking white men's spirits, many warriors beat their wives and killed one another.

The greed of the traders and the weakness of our warriors had brought this calamity on us. Despite laws against the sale of whiskey, white men hid their spirits in the woods when the tribe met at Fort Wayne. Many of our men could not resist the lure of the poison. After receiving their portion of the annuity, they would trade their silver for spirits and turn our gatherings into occasions for mindless brawling. In 1831 I relocated our council house to my land at the Forks of the Wabash. Thereafter, when my tribesmen met I kept bad white men from them. I allowed only honest traders on my land.

Yet the plight of my people grew even more desperate. In 1832 the American commissioners asked that we sell our remaining ground in exchange for land farther west. I refused their proposal. It was here that the Great Spirit had fixed our homes, and here our bones would remain. I believed the Great Spirit had made the western lands for the use of other tribes, and we did not belong there.

In 1834 the commissioners returned to make another treaty. I drove a good bargain. We received a large sum of money for a small amount of land. And titles to individual tracts were given to me and other chiefs. Again I refused removal west.

Then two years ago I signed another treaty. It included forty-three grants of land to tribal members. Through these grants the Miami still hold a portion of our ancestral ground. However, the government continues to insist we move west. Though I have not consented, I have sent a party of chiefs to inspect the land offered us.

I must soon commit my soul to the God who gave it and leave my earthly home. I will no longer be able to speak for my people. What will become of them? Only the Miami remain in Indiana. Can they continue to stand on the ground of our ancestors? If removed from the din of white civilization, might they better hear the ancestors' voices?

Chief Richardville's home in Fort Wayne, Indiana, was built for him by the United States government.

*I have watched and waited, and now I must act. With one final treaty I hope
to assure my tribe's survival. I pray for the wisdom to achieve this purpose.*

~ *Jean Baptiste Richardville (1840)*

In 1840 Chief Richardville drew up a treaty agreeing to the removal of the
Miami to a western reservation after five years. The treaty allowed
Richardville's family and other Miami with individual land grants to stay on
their lands. When the time for emigration arrived, about half of the tribe
removed to Kansas and half remained in Indiana.

At his death in 1841 Richardville was reputed to be the richest man in
Indiana and the wealthiest Indian in America. He owned nearly 6,000 acres
of land and three houses—one on his tract near Fort Wayne, one at the Forks
of the Wabash, and one near Peru, Indiana. His iron safe held gold and silver
worth $200,000. La Blonde, one of Richardville's daughters, married James
Godfroy, the son of another wealthy chief. Another daughter, Catherine, married Francis Lafontaine, who followed Richardville as chief of all the Miami in
Indiana.

Some fault Richardville for using his position as chief to gain wealth and
special privileges for his own family. Though his wealth caused some jealou-
sies, he was generally held in high esteem by his tribe. He was also respected
by white associates who vied to dine at his elegant home near Fort Wayne.

Richardville was a generous father figure who genuinely cared about
his tribe's welfare. Though he personally profited from his dealings with the
government, the chief's property was available to any tribesman in need.
Richardville's shrewd treaty dealings led to large annuities distributed to tribal
members and removal long after other tribes were forced west. In the end, his
strategy of gaining title to land for individual tribesmen resulted in nearly half
of the Miami remaining in Indiana, a truly remarkable achievement.

The Traders

When negotiating treaties Richardville had the support of powerful
allies—the traders. They gained as much as his tribe from large annuity payments. Richardville himself was a trader, like his Indian mother and French-
Canadian father. His parents' business had been largely based on the simple

exchange of furs for European goods. The traders offered the Indians blankets, kettles, guns, and whiskey. The Indians paid for these goods with furs.

As the Indians became more dependent on European products, the numbers of fur-bearing animals declined. Causes of decline included Indian overhunting as well as conversion of forest to farmland. Like white Americans, the Indians increasingly used silver coins, rather than furs, to pay for their purchases. They received the coins at annuity payment time. In effect the Indians traded their land for cash to buy goods from the traders. The more money the Indians received for their land, the more goods the traders could sell them. For this reason the traders became the Indians' greatest allies during treaty negotiations.

Ultimately the traders became a more powerful force for Indian decline and removal than all the armies of Long Knives. "Firewater" sold by greedy traders contributed to large-scale alcoholism among the Indians. The practice of selling goods on credit also accelerated the Indians' need to sell more land.

In 1803 President Thomas Jefferson wrote a private letter to Governor William Henry Harrison outlining his thoughts on Indian policy. He said: "We shall push our trading houses, and be glad to see the good and influential individuals among them run in debt, because we observe that when these debts get beyond what the individuals can pay, they become willing to lop them off by a cession of lands." Jefferson's vision of conquest by trade became a reality. The traders encouraged the Indians to run up huge debts. The government paid off the debts directly to the traders as payment for Indian land. The tribe only received the portion of the purchase price remaining after its debts were paid. As part of the 1832 treaty with the Potawatomi, the American government agreed to pay $62,412 to a long list of claimants. Money that could have enriched the tribe went to pay off the debts of individual tribesmen.

One large trading company was owned by brothers George and William Ewing. At first the Ewings supported Richardville's efforts to keep the tribe in Indiana. Miami tribesmen bought huge quantities of goods from the traders, and the Ewings wanted to keep their customers nearby. Once it became clear that the tribe would be leaving, they lost no time in profiting from the event.

In the summer of 1840 they quickly bought a huge stock of items for their store in Peru, Indiana. They sold them to Miami tribesmen on credit. Meanwhile the Ewings used their influence to help Richardville conclude his final treaty. The treaty set aside $300,000 for payment of debts. A large portion of this money went directly to the Ewings. By the time the treaty was signed

Major Miami Sites
circa 1847–1872

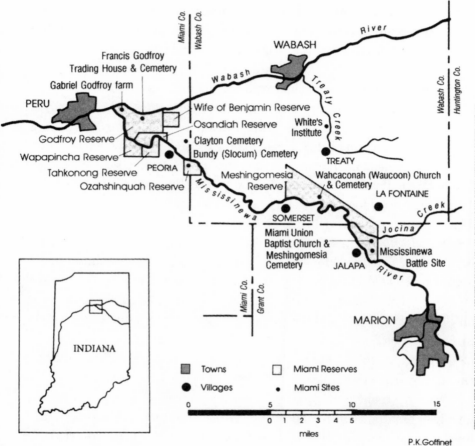

Land grants negotiated by Richardville and his successors secured a presence in Indiana for the Miami decades after the tribe's removal in 1846.

in November, the Ewings had sold more than $123,000 in goods. They sold another $140,000 worth of goods before the treaty was ratified three months later.

When time for the Miami removal arrived, the Ewings saw one last chance for profit. They contracted with the government to take the tribe west. William accompanied the Miami on their journey. In October 1846 the brokenhearted tribesmen boarded canal boats. Many clutched small bags of their native soil. Curious white spectators watched the sad procession pass by. At Cincinnati the Indians boarded a steamer to Saint Louis. From there another boat carried them up the Missouri River.

George met them for the final leg of their journey. On November 9, 323 Miamis arrived at their new reservation in Kansas. The Ewings and their partners received $140 for each Indian moved. The shrewd traders had made another nice sum at the expense of the Indians.

The American government sent its armies against the Indians many times. White settlers demanded more and more land and pressed for their removal. But in the end it was the traders who spurred the Indians' sale of land and carried them away to make way for American expansion.

Wares displayed at Conner Prairie Interactive History Park, show that trading posts served as a general store for Indians. They could buy items such as vases, tools, rifles, and any kind of other goods.

COURTESY OF CONNER PRAIRIE INTERACTIVE HISTORY PARK, FISHERS, INDIANA

Glossary

allies: Partners. In war, two or more groups fighting together against a common enemy. Indian tribes were often allied with the British against the American government.

annuity: A fixed amount of money paid to a person or group each year. Money paid to the Indian tribes for land ceded to the American government was usually in the form of an annuity paid to the chiefs by an Indian agent at a yearly gathering of tribesmen.

artillery: Large guns such as cannons, or the branch of the army that uses these weapons.

avenge: To do harm or inflict injury in return for a harm or injury; to get revenge.

bayonet: A sharp-pointed blade that is often attached to a rifle for use in close fighting.

black robes: A name used by Indians for Catholic priests.

blockhouse: A stockade or small fort made of logs where settlers gathered for protection.

cede: To give up or sign away something to another person or group. The Indian tribes ceded land to the American government in treaties.

cholera: A bacterial infection of the small intestines causing severe diarrhea and dehydration, spread through contaminated food and water. The first cholera outbreak in the United States was in 1832, brought across the ocean by European immigrants.

confederacy: League or partnership among groups of people who unite for a common cause. Indian tribes formed confederacies to fight the American army.

convert: A person who has been persuaded to adopt a new belief or practice.

cooper: A person who makes containers built of wooden staves such as barrels or buckets.

dragoons: Cavalry; military regiments on horseback.

emigration: The leaving of one's native land to settle in a new land.

Fifteen Fires: Indian term for the United States, which numbered fifteen states at the time of the Treaty of Greenville in 1795. When Tennessee became a state in 1796 the United States became "Sixteen Fires."

flatboat: A large rectangular flat-bottomed boat used on inland waterways, commonly used by pioneers moving west on the Ohio River. They could dismantle the boat at the end of their journey and use the planks to build a house.

gauntlet: A challenging test of strength, speed, and courage demanded of male captives of the Indians. The captive was forced to run between two long lines of Indians who struck them with rocks, sticks, and switches.

Glaize: Area of present-day northwest Ohio along the Maumee and Auglaize Rivers, where many Indians, especially the Shawnee, built their villages in the late 1700s. Indians of many tribes congregated there waiting to confront General Anthony Wayne's army.

gout: A disease causing painful inflammation of the joints, especially in the feet.

headwaters: The area at the source of a river; the place where it forms.

Indian agent: A representative of the government appointed to maintain good relations and further the government's goals in relation to the Indian tribes of an area. Some duties of American agents were promoting "civiliza-tion," facilitating peace among the various tribes, supervising government trading houses, and distributing annuity payments to the chiefs. The agents reported to the territorial governor and secretary of war.

Indiana Territory: Area carved out of the Northwest Territory in 1800, origi-nally including present-day Indiana, Illinois, Wisconsin, parts of Michigan and Minnesota, and a strip of Ohio.

Kekionga: A group of Indian villages near the confluence of the Maumee, Saint Marys, and Saint Joseph Rivers (site of present-day Fort Wayne, Indi-ana). Kekionga was considered the heart of the Miami tribal territory.

Long Knives: Name given to white military men by the Indians because of their use of swords or bayonets. From the time of the American Revolution onward the term referred more exclusively to American soldiers or frontiersmen.

massacre: Brutal murder of a group of people who have little means of defense.

militant: Aggressive, warlike, willing to fight.

militia: A detachment of armed men formed from the citizens of a town or state for its defense or to supplement a regular army's forces during an emergency.

missionary: A person who tries to convert others to his own religion or set of beliefs, usually in a region away from his native home.

Moravian Church: A Protestant denomination of Christianity known for its missionary work. After establishing settlements in North America in the 1740s, the Moravians conducted extensive missionary work to convert the Indians to Christianity.

neutrality: The stance of not joining one side or the other during a dispute or war, but staying out of the fight.

Northwest Territory, Old Northwest: Land west of Pennsylvania and northwest of the Ohio River, made up of the present-day states of Ohio, Indiana, Illinois, Michigan, Wisconsin, and northeastern Minnesota. After the Revolutionary War, the area was assigned to the United States by the British in the Treaty of Paris. The governance of the territory was set up by the Northwest Ordinance, enacted by Congress in 1787. The territory was dissolved in 1803 when Ohio became a state.

pacifist: A person who does not believe in using violence and refuses to go to war.

plunder: To loot or to take another's possessions by force or as spoils of war; the goods taken in this way.

prophet: A person who is thought to have unique spiritual powers and knowledge of the will of God. The special powers usually include the ability to predict or "prophesize" the course of future events.

Redcoats: Term used for British soldiers.

smallpox: Serious viral illness spread by personal contact and brought to the Americas by Europeans. Smallpox was especially deadly to the Indians because of their lack of previous exposure and natural immunity to the disease.

squatter: A person who settles on a property without any legal claim. Settlers would often build a home and begin farming on Indian or government land without first purchasing or gaining rights to it.

treaty: A formal agreement or contract between individuals or groups. A treaty after a war establishes the terms of peace, largely set forth by the victors and acceded to by the vanquished. Many treaties were brokered between the American government and the Indian tribes, exchanging Indian land for annuities and other goods and services provided by the government. To "treat" is to negotiate the terms of a treaty.

Bibliography

Allen, Carole M. et al., eds. "The Man in the Middle—Chief J. B. Richardville." *The Indiana Historian* (November 1993).

Allison, Harold. *The Tragic Saga of the Indiana Indians*. Paducah, KY: Turner Publishing Co., 1986.

Ankenbruck, John. *Voice of the Turtle*. Fort Wayne, IN: News Publishing, 1974.

Anson, Bert. *The Miami Indians*. Norman: University of Oklahoma Press, 1970.

Barr, Daniel P. "A Monster So Brutal: Simon Girty and the Degenerative Myth of the American Frontier," *Essays in History*, http://www.essaysinhistory.com/articles/2012/114.

Barrman, Floyd A., and J. Martin West. *St. Clair's Defeat*. [Ohio?]: Floyd A. Barrman and J. Martin West, supported by the Road to Greenville Grant of the Ohio Historical Society and the Fort Recovery Bicentennial Commission, 1991.

Battle of Fallen Timbers. Toledo, OH: Fallen Timbers Battlefield Preservation Commission, 1998. Videocassette (VHS), 18 min.

Baxter, Nancy Niblack. *The Miamis!* Indianapolis: Guild Press of Indiana, 1987.

Bial, Raymond. *The Shawnee*. Tarrytown, NY: Benchmark Books, 2004.

Bicentennial Heritage Trail Committee. *On the Heritage Trail, Fort Wayne, Indiana*. Fort Wayne: Arch, 1994.

Birzer, Bradley J. "French Imperial Remnants on the Middle Ground: The Strange Case of August de La Balme and Charles Beaubien." *Journal of the Illinois State Historical Society* (Summer 2000): 135–54.

Bodly, Temple. George Rogers Clark: His Life and Public Service. 8 vols. Cambridge, MA: Houghton Mifflin, 1926.

Bodurtha, Arthur L., ed. *History of Miami County Indiana*. Chicago: Lewis Publishing, 1914.

Bowen, Angela. *The Battle of Tippecanoe*, 3rd ed. Lafayette, IN: Tippecanoe County Historical Association, 2004.

Brice, Wallace A. *History of Fort Wayne, from the Earliest Known Accounts of This Point, to the Present Period*. Fort Wayne, IN: D. W. Jones & Son, Steam Book and Job Printers, 1868. Reprint, Salem, MA: Higginson Book Co., [1997?].

Calloway, John. *The Shawnees and the War for America*. New York: Viking Penguin, 2007.

Cantor, George. *North American Indian Landmarks*. Detroit: Visible Ink Press, 1993.

Carter, Harvey Lewis. *The Life and Times of Little Turtle: First Sagamore of the Wabash*. Urbana: University of Illinois Press, 1987.

Cave, Alfred. *Review of Blue Jacket: Warrior of the Shawnees*, by John Sugden. *Journal of the Illinois State Historical Society* (Summer 2001): 219–21.

Cayton, Andrew R. L. *Frontier Indiana*. Bloomington: Indiana University Press, 1996.

Corson, Dorothy V. "A Sacred Place Filled with Sacred Memories." Notre Dame, www.nd.edu/~wcawley/corson/logchapel.htm.

Cox, Sanford C. *Recollections of the Early Settlement of the Wabash Valley*. Lafayette, IN: Courier Steam Book and Job Printers, 1860. Reprint, Freeport, NY: Books for Libraries Press, 1970.

Cunningham, Maggi. *Little Turtle*. Minneapolis: Dillon Press, 1978.

Cushing, Caleb. *Outlines of the Life and Public Services, Civil and Military, of William Henry Harrison*. Boston: Eastburn's Press, 1840. Northern Illinois University Libraries Digitalization Projects, http://lincoln.lib.niu.edu/file.php?file=cushing.html.

Cwiklik, Robert. *Tecumseh: Shawnee Rebel*. New York: Chelsea House Publishers, 1995.

Drake, Benjamin. *Life of Tecumseh and of His Brother The Prophet; with a Historical Sketch of the Shawanoe Indians*. Cincinnati: E. Morgan & Co., 1850.

Dunn, Jacob Piatt. *True Indian Stories*. Indianapolis: Sentinel Printing, 1909.

Dye, Kitty. *Maconaquah's Story: The Saga of Frances Slocum*. Port Clinton, OH: LeClere Publishing Co., 1996.

Edmunds, R. David, ed. *Enduring Nations: Native Americans in the Midwest*. Urbana: University of Illinois Press, 2008.

_____. *The Shawnee Prophet*. Lincoln: University of Nebraska Press, 1983.

_____. *Tecumseh and the Quest for Indian Leadership*. New York: Addison Wesley Longman, 1984.

Eggleston, Edward, and Lillie Eggleston Seelye. *Tecumseh and the Shawnee Prophet*. New York: Dodd, Mead & Co., 1878.

Ericsson, Ann, and Dwight Ericsson, eds. *The Forks of the Wabash: An Historical Survey*. Huntington, IN: Historic Forks of the Wabash, 1990.

Esarey, Logan, ed. *Governors Messages and Letters. Vol. 1, William Henry Harrison (1800–1811)*. Indianapolis: Indiana Historical Commission, 1922.

_____. *A History of Indiana from Its Exploration to 1922*. Vol. 1. Dayton, OH: Dayton Historical Publishing, 1922.

"Fallen Timbers Battlefield," Metroparks of the Toledo Area, http://www.fallentimbersbattlefield.com/.

Feest, Christian F., R., David Edmunds, Sarah E. Cooke, and Rachel Ramadhyani. *Indians and a Changing Frontier: The Art of George Winter*. Indianapolis: Indiana Historical Society in cooperation with the Tippecanoe County Historical Association, 1993.

Flanagan, John K. "The Treaty of St. Louis and Black Hawk's Bitterness." *Northern Illinois University Law Review* 21, no. 2–3 (2001): 405–9, http://heinonline.org/.

Gaff, Alan D. *Bayonets in the Wilderness: Anthony Wayne's Legion in the Old Northwest*. Norman: University of Oklahoma Press, 2004.

Glenn, Elizabeth, and Stewart Rafert. *The Native Americans*. Indianapolis: Indiana Historical Society Press, 2009.

_____. "Native Americans." In *Peopling Indiana: The Ethnic Experience*. Edited by Robert M. Taylor and Connie A. McBirney. Indianapolis: Indiana Historical Society, 1996.

Godfroy, Chief Clarence. *Miami Indian Stories*. Winona Lake, IN: Light and Life Press, 1961.

Goebel, Dorothy Burne. *William Henry Harrison: A Political Biography*. Indianapolis: Historical Bureau of the Indiana Library and Historical Department, 1926.

Goehring, Susan. *Schoenbrunn: A Meeting of Cultures*. Columbus: Ohio Historical Society, 1997.

Griswold, Bert J. *Fort Wayne, Gateway of the West 1802–1813*. Indianapolis: Historical Bureau of the Indiana Library and Historical Department, 1927.

_____. *The Pictorial History of Fort Wayne Indiana*. Chicago: Robert O. Law, 1917.

Harrison, William Henry. *A Discourse on the Aborigines of the Ohio Valley*. Chicago: Fergus Printing, 1883.

Havighurst, Walter. *George Rogers Clark: Soldier in the West*. New York: McGraw-Hill, 1952.

Hay, Henry. *A Narrative of Life on the Old Frontier*. Edited by M. M. Quaife. Madison: State Historical Society of Wisconsin, 1915.

History of Allen County, Ohio. Chicago: Warner, Beers & Co., 1885.

History of Miami County, Indiana. Chicago: Brant & Fuller, 1887.

History of St. Joseph County, Indiana. Chicago: Chas. C. Chapman & Co., 1880.

History of Tuscarawas County, Ohio. Chicago: Warner, Beers & Co., 1884.

Holliday, Murray. *Battle of the Mississinewa, 1812*. Marion, IN: Grant County Historical Society, 1964.

Horsman, Reginald. "The British Indian Department and the Abortive Treaty of Lower Sandusky, 1793." *The Ohio Historical Quarterly* (July 1961): 189–213.

Howard, Timothy Edward. *A History of St. Joseph County, Indiana*. Vol. 2. Chicago: Lewis Publishing, 1907.

Hurt, R. Douglas. *The Ohio Frontier*. Bloomington: Indiana University Press, 1996.

Hutton, Paul A. "William Wells: Frontier Scout and Indian Agent." *Indiana Magazine of History* 74 (September 1978): 184–220.

Index to the Miscellaneous Documents of the House of Representatives for the Second Session of the Forty-Fifth Congress, 1877–78. Vol.1. Washington, DC: Government Printing Office, 1878.

"Indian Council of 1807," *The Ross County Historical Recorder* (Summer 2007): 4.

Jackson, Helen Hunt. *A Century of Dishonor: A Sketch of the United States Government's Dealings with Some of the Indian Tribes*. New York: Harper and Brothers, 1881.

Jackson, Stephen T. "Chief Anderson and His Legacy." Madison County Historical Society, http://mchs.yolasite.com/chief-anderson.php.

Jacobs, Charles M. *Wayne's Trace: Fort Deposit to Fort Industry*. Chicago: Arcadia Publishing, 2003.

Jung, Patrick J. *The Black Hawk War of 1832*. Norman: University of Oklahoma Press, 2008.

Kelley, Darwin. "Securing the Land: John Tipton and the Miami Indians." *Old Fort News* (January–June 1962).

Klinck, Carl F. *Tecumseh, Fact and Fiction in Early Records.* Englewood Cliffs, NJ: Prentice-Hall, 1961.

Knopf, Richard C., ed. *Anthony Wayne, a Name in Arms: Soldier, Diplomat, Defender of Expansion Westward of a Nation; the Wayne-Knox-Pickering-McHenry Correspondence.* Pittsburgh: University of Pittsburgh Press, 1959.

Knudson, Douglas M. *Tippecanoe Battlefield.* Lawrenceburg, IN: The Creative Co., 1997.

Lake, Martin. *The Mississineway Expedition.* Grant County Historical Society, 1997.

Larson, John Lauritz, and David G. Vanderstel. "Agent of Empire: William Conner on the Indiana Frontier, 1800-1805." *Indiana Magazine of History* 80 (December 1984): 301—28.

Line, Sarah Jane. "The Indians on the Mississinewa." *Indiana Magazine of History* 9 (September 1913): 187–94.

Lockridge, Ross F. "History on the Mississinewa." *Indiana Magazine of History* 30 (March 1934): 29–56.

"Logan, James." In *American National Biography.* 24 vols. New York: Oxford University Press, 1999– .

Madison, James H. *The Indiana Way.* Bloomington: Indiana University Press, 1986.

"Matthew Elliott." Ohio History Central, http://www.ohiohistorycentral.org/entry.php?rec=147.

McKee, Alexander." Dictionary of Canadian Biography Online, University of Toronto, 2000, http://www.biographi.ca/009004-119.01-e.php?&id_nbr=2062.

McKee, Irving. "The Centennial of the Trail of Death," *Indiana Magazine of History* 35 (March 1939): 27–41.

McPherson, Alan J., and James Carr. *Notable American Indians: Indiana and Adjacent States.* Bloomington, IN: Author House, 2007.

Meginness, John Franklin. *Biography of Frances Slocum, the Lost Sister of Wyoming: A Complete Narrative of Her Captivity and Wanderings among the Indians.* Williamsport, PA: Heller Bros.' Printing House, 1891.

Meisch, Sarah A., "1780 Battle Site Commemorated," *Fort Wayne Journal Gazette*, November 6, 2005.

Millett, Allan R. "Caesar and the Conquest of the Northwest Territory: The Harrison Campaign, 1811." *Timeline* 14, no. 4 (July/August 1997): 2–19.

_____. "Caesar and the Conquest of the Northwest Territory: The Second Harrison Campaign, 1813." *Timeline* 14, no. 5 (September/October 1997): 2–21.

Mollenkopf, Jim. *The Great Black Swamp II: More Historical Tales of Northwestern Ohio.* Toledo, OH: Lake of the Cat Publishing, 2001.

Montgomery, H. *The Life of Major-General William H. Harrison, Ninth President of the United States.* Cleveland: Tooker and Gatchell, 1852.

Moore, Frank. *American Eloquence: A Collection of Speeches and Addresses, by the Most Eminent Orators of America; with Biographical Sketches and Illustrative Notes.* Vol. 2. New York: D. Appleton and Co., 1857.

Murphy, David Thomas. *Murder in Their Hearts: The Fall Creek Massacre*. Indianapolis: Indiana Historical Society Press, 2010.

Myers, Albert Cook, ed. *William Penn's Own Account of the Lenni Lenape or Delaware Indians*. Wilmington, DE: Middle Atlantic Press, 1970.

Nardo, Don. *The Indian Wars: From Frontier to Reservation*. San Diego: Lucent Books, 2002.

Nelson, Larry. *Fort Meigs: War of 1812 Battleground*. Columbus: Ohio Historical Society, 1999.

Nelson, Larry L. "Cultural Mediation, Cultural Exchange, and the Invention of the Ohio Frontier." *Ohio History* 105 (Winter–Spring 1996): 72–91.

Nichols, Roger L. *Black Hawk and the Warrior's Path*. Arlington Heights, IL: Harlan Davidson, 1992.

Olmstead, Earl P. "A Day of Shame: The Gnadenhutten Story," *Timeline 8*, no. 4 (August/September 1991): 20–33.

Patrick, Jeff L., ed. "'We Lay There Doing Nothing': John Jackson's Recollection of the War of 1812." *Indiana Magazine of History* 88 (June 1992): 111–31.

Poinsatte, Charles. *Outpost in the Wilderness: Fort Wayne, 1706–1828*. Fort Wayne, IN: Allen County, Fort Wayne Historical Society, 1976.

Pokagon, Simon. "The Massacre of Fort Dearborn at Chicago." *Harper's New Monthly Magazine* 98 (1899): 649–56.

"Population of the United States." *American Quarterly Register* 6, no. 1 (August 1833): 2–13.

Potterf, Rex M. *William Henry Harrison Protector of Fort Wayne*. N.p., [195–].

"Private Nathaniel Vernon, Pittsburgh Blues." In *The War of 1812 in Person: Fifteen Accounts by United States Army Regulars, Volunteers, and Militiamen*. Edited by John C. Fredriksen. Jefferson, NC: McFarland & Co., 2010.

Prucha, Francis Paul. *American Indian Treaties*. Berkeley: University of California Press, 1994.

Rafert, Stewart. *The Miami Indians of Indiana: A Persistent People, 1654–1994*. Indianapolis: Indiana Historical Society, 1996.

———. "Ozahshinquah." *Traces of Indiana and Midwestern History* 4, no. 2 (Spring 1992): 4–11.

Raynor, Keith. "The Battle of Mississinewa 1812," The War of 1812 Website, www.warof1812.ca/mississa.htm.

Roberts, Bessie K. *Fort Wayne: The Frontier Post*. Fort Wayne, IN: Public Library of Fort Wayne and Allen County, 1965.

Robertson, Robert S. et al. *The Valley of the Upper Maumee River*. Madison, WI: Democrat Printing, 1889.

Rohr, Martha E. *Historical Sketch of Fort Recovery*. Fort Recovery, OH: Fort Recovery Historical Society, 1991.

Rugeley, Terry. "Savage and Statesman: Changing Historical Interpretations of Tecumseh." *Indiana Magazine of History* 85 (December 1989): 289–311.

Simonis, Louis A. *Maumee River, 1835*. Defiance, OH: Defiance County Historical Society, 1979.

Sloat, Bill. "Blue Jacket Was Indian, Not White, DNA Shows: Legend Surrounding Fierce Chief's History Not Based on Reality." *Cleveland Plain Dealer*, April 13, 2006.

Sugden, John. *Blue Jacket: Warrior of the Shawnees.* Lincoln: University of Nebraska Press, 2000.

———. *Tecumseh: A Life.* New York: Henry Holt, 1997.

Taylor, Robert M., Jr. et al. *Indiana: A New Historical Guide.* Indianapolis: Indiana Historical Society, 1989.

Thompson, Charles N. *Sons of the Wilderness: John and William Conner.* Indianapolis: Indiana Historical Society, 1937. Reprint, Noblesville, IN: Conner Prairie Press, 1988

Thornbrough, Gayle, ed. *Letter Book of the Indian Agency at Fort Wayne, 1809–1815.* Indianapolis: Indiana Historical Society, 1961.

Tippecanoe County Historical Society, "Tippecanoe Battlefield," http://www.tcha.mus.in.us/battlefield.htm

Troyer, Byron L. *Yesterday's Indiana.* Miami: E. A. Seemann Publishing, 1975.

Van Voorhis Wendler, Marilyn. *The Kentucky Frontiersman, the Connecticut Yankee, and Little Turtle's Granddaughter: A Blending of Cultures.* Westminster, MD: Heritage Books, 2007.

Warren, Stephen. *The Shawnees and Their Neighbors, 1795–1870.* Urbana: University of Illinois Press, 2005.

White, Richard. *The Middle Ground: Indians, Empires, and Republics in the Great Lakes Region, 1650–1916.* New York: Cambridge University Press, 1991.

Whitson, Rolland Lewis, ed. *Centennial History of Grant County Indiana, 1812–1912.* Chicago: Lewis Publishing, 1914.

Woehrmann, Paul. *At the Headwaters of the Maumee.* Indianapolis: Indiana Historical Society, 1971.

Young, Calvin M. *Little Turtle (Me-she-kin-no-quah): The Great Chief of the Miami Indian Nation.* Greenville, OH: Calvin M. Young, 1917.

Zeisberger, David. *Excerpts from the Diary of The Reverend David Zeisberger, 1772–1777.* Excerpted and Introduced by Daniel R. Porter III. Columbus: Ohio Historical Society, 1972.

Index of Names